Best w

Margaret C. Jones.

She Spied
FOR FREEDOM

She Spied
FOR FREEDOM

MARY RICHARDS
A BLACK
CIVIL WAR
AGENT

MARGARET C. JONES

FONTHILL

Fonthill Media Language Policy

Fonthill Media publishes in the international English language market. One language edition is published worldwide. As this publication focuses on historical events that took place in the United States, American English has been adopted.

www.fonthill.media
office@fonthillmedia.com

First published in the United Kingdom
and the United States of America 2024

British Library Cataloguing in Publication Data:
A catalogue record for this book is available from the British Library

ISBN 978-1-78155-919-2

Typeset in 10.5pt on 13pt Sabon
Printed and bound in England

For my sister Joanna

Preface

At the start of the American Civil War, an educated young black woman came to work in the home of Jefferson Davis, president of the rebel Southern Confederacy. Posing as an illiterate slave, she spent years drudging for the Davis family, while gathering intelligence vital to the cause of the Union. Her motive for putting her life in danger was to help in the fight for freedom for all those held in Southern slavery.

I first heard of Mary Richards while doing research for a different book, about women working undercover. Mary's legend—often given inaccurately under the name of "Mary Bowser"—is all over the internet, in a tangle of myths and tall tales that make it hard at times to sort fact from fiction. This book aims to set the record straight.

It tells of Mary's remarkable early life—of a child born into slavery and given her freedom, in order to spend four years as a teenage missionary in West Africa—and of her time in the "White House of the Confederacy," where she performed such valuable service for the Union. It tells what we know about her life after the war, in the dangerous work of teaching freed slaves in Reconstruction Georgia. It is also the story of the people she lived with, and who shaped her world—her patron Elizabeth Van Lew; those, like Jefferson Davis and his wife, she dealt with in the camp of the enemy; her allies in the Richmond spy ring; and the people whose goodwill she came to depend on after the war.

I have always been drawn to histories of exceptional, brave individuals—people who, like the war hero and former slave in this story, defy stereotypes and confound society's expectations of them. Richards was from a humble background, born into a time and place where her race was despised; yet she played her part in helping the Union win the Civil War.

She Spied for Freedom tells of a heroic journey through an often hostile world. Mary Richards was a lone warrior for justice who faced poverty, illness, isolation, brutal racism, and life-threatening danger—and never surrendered.

Acknowledgments

The name of a single author on the cover of a book like this one almost always conceals a collaborative effort. Almost any biography owes its existence to the labors of archivists, journalists, and fellow historians over the course of years. Warmest thanks are due, therefore, to the many who have aided my research for *She Spied for Freedom*. There are the custodians of priceless records of the past: Family Search; the National Archives and Records Administration (NARA); the Harriet Beecher Stowe Center, Hartford, Connecticut; the Imperial War Museum, UK; the Library of Virginia; and the Schlesinger Library on the History of Women in America at the Radcliffe Institute, Harvard. The book would be the poorer without its illustrations, for which I am most grateful to the American Battlefield Trust, the American Civil War Museum, the British Library, Hawaiian Mission Houses Historic Site and Archives, the Library of Congress (many times over), the Missouri History Museum, the Virginia Department of Historic Resources, and the Robert W. Woodruff Library, Clark Atlanta University. I also wish to thank John Shuck, who guided me to the location of Mary Richards' graveyard memorial in the Woodland Cemetery, Richmond.

Two scholars in the fields of nineteenth-century history have been especially helpful in developing my initial interest in the story of Mary Richards. One is a distinguished scholar among the nation's leading authorities on African-American culture and history, Professor Darlene Hine, who has inspired research on lost figures in Black History, including the mysterious "Mary Bowser." The other is Professor Lois Leveen, whose tireless work on unearthing new information about "the vanishing black woman spy" has yielded much that was previously unknown. I owe an unpayable debt to them both.

Warm thanks are due to the editors at Fonthill—Alan Sutton, Jasper Hadman, Jamie Hardwick, Jay Slater—for your faith in this project, for helping me see it through to the finish, and to Fonthill's supportive marketing and other staff. I would be nowhere without you.

I am deeply grateful also to those among my friends who over the months have listened patiently while I held forth about my fascination with Mary Richards. The enthusiasm you expressed for my latest hobbyhorse has kept me going through many long hours of work. Professor Essam el Din Fattouh, my husband of half a lifetime, has been particularly supportive. He listened attentively while I read him the entire first draft of this book, and made a number of valuable suggestions, drawing on his long experience as a literary critic.

Finally, there is the debt I owe to African-American friends, colleagues, and students at Purdue University, and in Washington State. Over the years they have patiently educated me, not only about the past of their people—by turns tragic, inspiring, and hopeful—but about the scars left by that past on contemporary African-American lives. It has been a sobering, valuable education. I hope I may have benefited from it in the writing of this book.

Contents

A Survivor

This young woman ... was now sent for; she came, and for a time was coached and trained for her mission; then ... she was installed as a waitress in the White House of the Confederacy.[1]

Huddled in farm wagons, struggling for breath under loads of hay, or trudging by night along lightless forest paths, lone men and women and whole families are on the move. Bent under bundles, they hobble on blistered feet. Older children stagger along under the weight of a younger brother or sister. Barefoot or shod, hungry and weary, they plod on, fording streams and splashing through rivers, dodging Confederate patrols, straining their ears for movement in the undergrowth or the dreaded sound of baying dogs. The people are slipping north to find the Union lines. It is a journey, always hard and dangerous, that grows easier as federal troops converge on Virginia. In the space of four years, half a million will take the road to freedom.

Some time towards the end of 1864, a young, free black woman in her twenties joins the straggling trail of fugitives. She is on her way to Fredericksburg, 60 miles from her birthplace in Richmond. Mary Richards has an especially urgent need to get out of Richmond. If the Confederate authorities find out what she has been doing there the last few years, her life will be over.

Mary Jane Richards. Mary Jane Henley. Mary Jones. Mary Bowser. Later to be called Richmonia St. Pierre. Mary Garvin. Mary Denman. She has been, or will be, known by all of these names. She has been a schoolgirl in the North, a teenage missionary in Africa, and more recently, a spy. In her chameleon existence she's learned to adapt to circumstances, living by her wits and on her own resources, in a world where every new situation seems more peculiar than the last, and nothing stays the same for long.

The constant shifts are at least partly a function of the changing times. The first decades of her life have seen the founding of a new state in Africa that welcomes African-American settlers, and a devastating civil war that will transform the world of the South forever. Mary has lived through these turbulent years, not as a passive spectator, but playing an active part. To understand how she ended up a secret agent in the household of the head of the rebel government during the American Civil War, we need to go back twenty-four years—to the time of Mary's birth.

"Who were her people?" In any biography, that question refers to someone's ancestry—first and foremost to her parents. In the case of an African-American slave, however, the answer is all too often cloaked in obscurity. A child might have been torn away from her family—sold, with as little concern as if she were a lamb or a calf, to a new master. Or her parentage might have been hidden to protect some powerful white person, to cover up scandal. Mary Richards was therefore not alone among African Americans in giving contradictory accounts of who her "people" were. To important whites, when asked, she might say her mother was a white woman, her father of Spanish and African descent. Or she would tell them that she did not know, which was more likely the case. At her baptism, the parish register described her simply as "a child belonging to Mrs. [Eliza] Van Lew." That mark of possession as a chattel is the only certain tie we have to Mary's origins. Beyond that, only members of the Van Lew family—Eliza, her daughter Elizabeth, and possibly a handful of others in the immediate household—could have identified the child's parents. Elizabeth's cousin Anna Whitlock claimed that Mary's mother was a cook named Caroline, hired out to the Van Lews on a temporary basis. That might have explained why the child remained with the white family; if Caroline could not easily have cared for her baby, the wealthy Van Lews might have offered to keep the child.[2]

Since Mary was baptized under the surname Richards, the evidence points to some unknown member of the Richards branch of the Van Lew family, as the child's father. This would presumably have made the Van Lews the de facto owners of the slave child. The theory that Mary's father was a Van Lew relative is given substance by Eliza's choice to have Mary baptized, not in the First African Baptist church less than a mile from the Van Lew's Church Hill mansion, where most blacks were christened, but in the elite St. John's Episcopal, the church of privileged white people. (Although, as will shortly be seen, there is another possible explanation for that decision.) Historic St. John's was where Richmond's wealthy attended on Sundays. It was the church where the American revolutionary Patrick

Henry had famously called for secession from Britain—"Give me Liberty or Give Me Death"—at the start of the Revolutionary War.

In most respects, the family in Richmond, Virginia, who in the eyes of the law were Mary's owners from the moment of her birth, lived no differently from others of their social class. Their mansion, in the select community of Church Hill, was an imposing white building, with a columned portico surmounting a flight of steps that led down into an expanse of garden. In the mansion's high-ceilinged rooms, guests dined off fine china as they discussed the issues of the day. In summer, the family, in company with other well-to-do Richmond citizens, traveled out of the city to "take the waters" at a nearby spa. They performed their duties as wealthy Christians by visiting the sick and giving alms to the "deserving poor." As a young woman, their daughter Elizabeth, like other Southern young ladies from wealthy families, had her share of parties and receptions, where she was introduced to potential husbands. With her neat, petite figure and blonde good looks, she was considered a beauty—expected to "marry well." (In fact, she would remain single all her life.)

Though so similar to their neighbors in much of their lifestyle, John and Eliza Van Lew differed from most of them in one important respect: unlike many in Richmond's business class, the couple had intellectual interests. Every year they spent large sums on books to extend their already substantial library. They read travel narratives, novels, works on politics and history. They loved to talk about their reading in the evenings, when Eliza's husband John came back from a day of overseeing business at his hardware stores in the city. They were on socializing terms with all the foremost families of Richmond, but also hosted receptions for writers and musicians. The poet Edgar Allen Poe and the famous operatic soprano Jenny Lind came to their home as honored guests. Elizabeth would become friends with the Swedish abolitionist and feminist author Fredrika Bremer, who, like the American abolitionist Anna Dickinson, stayed with the Van Lews when she visited Richmond.

This was the atmosphere in which little enslaved Mary Richards was growing up. As she ran errands and did chores for the white people who controlled her life, the book-lined shelves and overheard intellectual discussion—even if she did not understand all of it—could have conveyed to her that culture and, above all, literacy were important.

Eliza's husband John Van Lew, born and raised in slave-owning Jamaica, had no problems of conscience about slavery. As he built his business into a wealthy enterprise, coming to own not only a chain of stores, but a farm outside the city, his purchase of human beings to serve in his household and shops and work his land only enhanced his social status among Richmond's upper class.

His wife, though, had always felt uncomfortable about owning fellow human beings. Eliza's father, a popular several times re-elected mayor of Philadelphia, had been a lifelong member of the Pennsylvania Abolition Society. After her husband John's death in 1843, the Van Lew family's continuing ownership of slaves increasingly troubled Eliza's conscience.

After years of soul-searching, she came to her decision. John had given instructions in his will that the twenty-one enslaved people he owned at the end of his life should be retained as property, to be handed down through the family. Eliza now decided to disobey his wishes. She told the family slaves that, whatever the law might say about it, in her eyes they were free. They might stay with the family as paid servants, or leave and go wherever they pleased. Either from loyalty, or because they saw the Van Lew women as considerate employers—or possibly because they had nowhere else to go—most of them opted to stay with the family. One of the first to be told she was a free person was the child Mary Richards, then no more than six or seven years old.

The repressive laws of Virginia, where slavery was concerned, in practice made it difficult and costly for a slave owner to free a slave. The process always involved recourse to the courts. It seems likely, therefore, that the Van Lews freed their slaves only in a private agreement—a practical arrangement that was never ratified in law. It was an ambiguous situation that would create difficulties for Mary in her adult life, but would also turn out to have surprising advantages.

Eliza Van Lew and her daughter had grown fond of Mary—this lively, talkative child. Mary was particularly loved by Elizabeth, for whom, as we shall see, the little girl was a servant, but also something of a household pet. And Elizabeth, being the kind of person she was, seems to have regarded her, too, as a work in progress, a project—someone to be shaped and developed according to a preordained program.

Elizabeth, twenty years Mary's senior, was to Mary a mistress, employer, mentor, patron, and benefactor—but also the only mother figure she would ever know. All the same, having never been quite a full member of the Van Lew family, Mary, even as an adult living far away from Richmond, always addressed Elizabeth in her letters as "Miss Bet."

Both Elizabeth and her mother soon recognized Mary's keen intelligence: her way with language, her quickness of understanding. She had, too, as it would later be said of her, an unusually good memory. It was clear to the Van Lews that if she were to live forever in their house as a domestic doing manual chores, her potential would be wasted. She needed scope for using her mind. The Van Lew women would therefore prepare her for something more challenging, more "ladylike," than domestic service; but also, as they saw it, more useful to society at large. They were going to send her away.

The Baptist church, where most black people in Richmond were baptized, would not christen a child until he or she reached the age of at least eight or nine, when they were deemed mature enough to understand the choice they were making. On May 17, 1846, Mary was only six—below the age of consent for christening by the Baptists. But the St. John's Episcopal church, where the Van Lew family themselves worshiped, was happy to baptize anyone from infancy upwards. In the following year, the Van Lews were going to send Mary to the North, "to gain an education," and the Van Lew women, devout Protestant Christians as they were, were not going to send a child out into the perils and snares of the world without the blessing of a church to protect her.

So it was that, at the advanced age of seven, Mary traveled north to the care of trusted Presbyterian friends in Princeton, New Jersey. She would develop her young mind by attending school. After this, they would prepare her for the role in life that they had chosen for her, whether she wanted it or not.

2

Missionaries

God has gracious designs for Africa.

—Alexander Crummell, African-American
missionary to Liberia[1]

When it came to finding a path in life, there were not so many options in the nineteenth century for a young black girl like Mary. While a few years of schooling in the North might seem to open the way for her, even there, her choices would in reality be very limited. For one thing, it would be illegal for her to go back to Virginia as a free black person who had received such Northern training. (There *were* free black people in Richmond. If they had skills, or were otherwise deemed economically useful, the authorities tended to look the other way and disregard the law, so that by 1860 as much as one-third of Virginia's black population was free.) But a clever young black female with too much education would find it hard to fit comfortably into her expected role as a household drudge or farm worker. Even in the North, her life would have been a struggle.

Evidently, Mary's patrons had recognized the problem and had come up with what, at the time, must have seemed to them an ingenious solution. It had been explained to Mary, even as they sent the seven-year-old off to school for the first time, that her destiny, once her schooling was done, was to leave America altogether and become a missionary overseas. But first she had to gain an education.

In the 1840s, the long row of terraced houses fronting the town cemetery on Princeton's Witherspoon Street, and the few side streets running off this main thoroughfare, formed the hub of the town's black community. It was an area of tanneries and slaughterhouses, where black people filled the dirty, heavy, unpleasant jobs that whites refused to do. Or they were porters and cleaners in Princeton's hotels and private houses, or in the College of New Jersey (later to be called Princeton University), a mile away from Witherspoon. As the area gained in prosperity in the 1850s, small shops and working men's cafés sprang up along the main street, serving those who lived in the modest timber-framed houses.

In May 1855, just a few months after Mary Richards had finished her education and left Princeton, a white abolitionist writer came to Witherspoon Street on a tour of inspection. Ann Maria Davison had been warned not to go. White friends and acquaintances had assured her that the residents of Witherspoon Street were "a poor miserable degraded set of beings, improvident, living from hand to mouth, all congregated together" in so-called "Negro Town." Davison saw fit to question these opinions, based on her own impressions of the few black people she had so far met in Princeton: "I had observed my washerwoman at the Hotel to be respectable in her deportment, neat and clean in her appearance—also the waiter at the Hotel where I was staying, was polite and civil, and altogether a very decent man." She had noticed a group of black schoolchildren in the street, "dressed well, deporting themselves as well as white children, with their school bags on their arms, seeming to contain a goodly number of books." None of these encounters appeared to square at all with what she had been told by the white Princetonians. She decided to check out the black neighborhood for herself, and "sallied forth" to find Witherspoon Street.[2]

She stopped to ask the way of a group of students. They were young white men from the Southern states who flatly disapproved of her plan to visit the black community. She would, they told her, "disgrace" herself, "as no decent ladies ever went among such filthy low people."

The students failed to put her off, however. Undaunted, Davison went on her way. Her aim went beyond mere voyeurism or touristic curiosity. She was on a mission—to disprove the common prejudice of the time that depicted blacks as inferiors, unable to care or provide for themselves, who needed to be kept as slaves for their own good. Since those who entertained such rationalizations for slavery refused to question their attitudes, Davison would do it for them.

She worked her way along Green Street, a side road adjoining Witherspoon's main thoroughfare, knocking on doors. At each, she asked the residents if she might come in and look at their living room. A total stranger barging into one's private space like this might, one would expect, have received short shrift. But Davison was made welcome. Once she explained the purpose of her visit, people on the whole seemed pleased to show her their modest dwellings. She went into fourteen in all. There were only two, she reported, "into which I could not go." (She does not say why.)

Some of the homes were tidy, Davison remarked. Others were in a bit of a mess. Things "were not in very good order," she reported of one house. (She had not exactly given the occupants notice of her coming, or any time to tidy up.) But even in the less tidy homes, there seemed to be plenty of bedding, "and all kinds of furniture to be comfortable." In every house, Davison saw "a Bible, sofa, handsome chairs, carpets, with ornamental little things which composed the parlor furniture," with a sideboard "and other suitable articles" in dining rooms.

Having assumed the people would all be illiterate, she was pleasantly surprised to find writing materials in most households. One older single lady had newspapers in her living room and a collection of religious books. She was invited into the home of a mailman, whose daughters all did handicrafts, and one of whom played the piano. Davison contrasted the modest comfort of these homes with the bare slave cabins she had seen on the plantations in her native Louisiana, furnished with no more than a sleeping bunk and a stool. In the report she wrote later, she set forth her findings about the black community of Princeton, "to shew that these poor miserable people (as they were called) live in their own comfortable homes, with no one to control them, or make them afraid." That she found it necessary to tell skeptical whites that people of even modest means, regardless of their ethnicity, could read and write, and owned books and furniture, speaks volumes about the ignorant prejudices then prevailing about the customs and capacities of blacks.

These self-respecting, hard-working residents of Witherspoon Street and its surroundings would form Mary's community—her family, even—for the next eight years. She would go to church with them on Sundays and attend school with their children. Very likely, young as she was, she stayed and was looked after in someone's home.

The Witherspoon Street church, which lay at the heart of Witherspoon's world, had been founded in 1835. Eighty black members had left a white-dominated place of worship, the First Presbyterian church on Nassau Street, where it seems they no longer felt welcome. Many now sent their children to what would later become the "Witherspoon Street School for Colored Children," run by the new black Presbyterian church.

The place for Mary's education had evidently been carefully chosen by the Van Lews with a view to their long-term plan for her. The whole Presbyterian community in Princeton in the 1800s, both white and black, was deeply engaged in missionary work. White male graduates of the Princeton Theological Seminary, like Robert Hamill and Edwin Williams, followed up their studies by traveling to preach the gospel overseas. And there were strong Presbyterian links with the College of New Jersey. That evangelical fervor was very much alive, too, in the black church and school of Witherspoon Street. Before the Civil War, even in the North, there were only a few centers of African-American education like the Witherspoon Street church, and this at a time when the evangelical call was coming loud and clear. At first, most missionaries who traveled abroad were men, many of them white male graduates of theological schools or universities. But a growing number of black, largely self-taught missionaries now began going forth to "convert the heathen."

There was even a handful of black female missionaries—two of whom were well known in Witherspoon Street. Witherspoon residents would certainly have heard about the courageous Cecilia Van Tyne and her work in Liberia. In 1841, Miss Van Tyne had gone to the new colony in West Africa, founded to serve as a home for former slaves, and helped to establish a new Presbyterian mission at Settra Kroo, a settlement on the coast. When her male fellow missionaries fell ill and died, Cecilia refused to be recalled home, and carried on at Settra Kroo, teaching and preaching on her own. Only when, three years later, she too succumbed to fever, did she leave Liberia. She came back to Princeton to teach the young children of Witherspoon Street, before setting out again four years later to work in Brazil.

Princeton's black community was passionate about education. While college entrance was denied to blacks, that was not going to stop them teaching the younger generation, and gaining all the knowledge they could for themselves. Their school at the black Presbyterian church had begun as a Sunday school, but quickly became a day school, with opportunities for students to gain more than narrowly focused religious learning. The children enrolled there acquired literacy, but also were able to study mathematics, literature, and history. By 1858, the school, which had till then run on an informal basis, had sixty-eight students on its books, and was formally established.

The school's head was another former missionary—the strong, intellectually gifted and compassionate Betsey Stockton, who was largely responsible for its founding. Like Mary, Stockton had been born into slavery—given as a child to Elizabeth and Ashbel Green. A Presbyterian minister, who later became president of the College of New Jersey, Dr. Green was a believer in the gradual abolition of the slave system. While employing Betsey as a servant in his household, he educated her to the same level as his own children. By the time she reached adulthood, she had become a "born-again" full member of the First Presbyterian church, and a free woman. In 1822, believing she had a vocation as a missionary, she set out with a group of like-minded others, to preach in the Sandwich Islands in the Pacific. She returned after four years, and from the 1830s onwards, dedicated herself to the education of the African-American children of Princeton.

Everyone in the black community, and white people around Princeton too, respected Betsey Stockton. One Princeton resident who had known her since childhood remembered her with particular admiration. In a brief tribute to her memory published in the *Pacific Commercial Advertiser*, he wrote that her "example and counsel" won her "the respect and regard of the whole town.... Among her own people she moved a queen and her word was law."[3] Many years later, he still treasured her portrait:

> I still have her picture, given to me by herself, with her turban as she always wore it, her strong but placid face and her portly form. Her manner was deliberate and dignified and by the younger people she was both loved and feared. Among the older people her influence was supreme.

Stockton lived in a single-story house in the heart of the black community, near the corner of Witherspoon and Green Street. "The grounds and building were always neat and attractive," wrote her biographer, and the interior of the house was "a model of cleanliness and order."

Stockton was still teaching Richmond's black students in the years after the Civil War, when she was in her seventies. An account of a government inspection of her school was full of praise:

> The superintendent and visitors of the public schools unhesitatingly state that, in their inspections, they found no school better trained, better instructed, or with evidence of greater success than hers.

Betsey Stockton would surely have been a powerful and inspiring role model for any young black girl—not least for one as intelligent and impressionable as Mary Richards.

The little world surrounding the church and school on Witherspoon Street became a center, not only of childhood education, but of debate and discussion about issues of concern to adults too—about the fugitive slave laws; about how white people used and abused biblical teachings to justify holding slaves; on the right of black people to have the vote and how to gain it (or rather, regain it, since in the early years of New Jersey, free blacks had been able to vote); and on the "return to Africa" movement. In her seven years growing up in this intellectually lively environment, young Mary listened and learned.

Along with a secular education, Betsey Stockton instilled in her students a fervent piety that was expected to show itself in good works. If you were truly a Christian, she told her students, you had to do something to "give back" to the world. You had a duty to serve God and your fellow human beings.

In the context of the fervent evangelizing Presbyterianism of Princeton and the examples of such heroic women preachers and teachers as Stockton and Van Tyne, Elizabeth's plans for her protégée Mary look less eccentric—certainly less exceptional—than they otherwise might. Like Betsey Stockton and Cecilia Van Tyne, Mary needed to find—or to have someone find for her—a suitable niche in life, and this in a white-dominated world that sometimes even questioned whether black people were fully human, let alone able to develop and apply their intellect.

What Mary herself thought about her assigned role as a missionary—whether the young girl, still in her early teens when she left Princeton, had any sense of an evangelical vocation—we do not know. By her own account, when told by the Van Lew women that she was "destined for a missionary's life in Africa," she had unquestioningly accepted it as her fate.[4]

Whether her new role was one she would have chosen for herself or not, the day arrived when Mary's education came to an end. In December 1855, her Princeton schooling was over. It was time for her to set out on her evangelical career. She was just fifteen.

She had said goodbye to Princeton, the town with its close-knit black community that had become her second home, and to school friends she would not see again for many years. It must have felt like a drastic rift with that familiar life. One imagines her anxious about the strange and possibly frightening new world she was sailing to. Did she also feel excited, though, at embarking on this new adventure?

The field of endeavor chosen for Mary was Liberia, the colony founded only thirty-four years before as a homeland for former slaves, and recognized for the past eight years, since 1847, as a proudly independent young nation. It was where Cecilia Van Tyne had worked as a missionary (and, Mary might have remembered also, where two of Cecilia's co-workers had met their deaths).

The idea of Liberia had originally been proposed as a possible solution to the alleged "problem" of what do about freed black slaves in America. With breathtaking simple-mindedness, the racist white elites of America had come up with their colonization project. Black people—regardless of whether they had been born in America, or for how many generations they had lived there—had, it was said, originally come from Africa. Why not send them back there? The fifth U.S. president, James Monroe (1758–1831), had supported the Liberia scheme, and the nation's capital, Monrovia, is named after him. A new organization, the American Colonization Society, was founded to promote the emigration idea, and to assist willing would-be colonists to cope with the challenges of moving overseas.

The project grew popular among various sectors of American society, albeit for different reasons. Idealistic Quakers hoped to see African Americans freed from slavery, living their own lives and prospering in a land they could call their own. Anxious slaveholders, who—even before the Civil War—feared revolts and revenge attacks from liberated slaves, wanted the small but growing numbers of freed black people to go and live anywhere but in America. "Their friends and their foes both desire [their] removal," one would-be emigrant wrote dryly of the largely white-inspired Liberia scheme.[5]

Many African Americans, including most anti-slavery campaigners, opposed the Liberia scheme in its entirety, with its underlying assumption that American-born black people had no right to live in the land of their birth. And, regardless of motive, no supporter of the colonization project seemed too concerned that the land identified as the site of the new colony was not exactly empty space, but already inhabited by indigenous Africans.

As for the prospects for those who considered moving to live there, whether Liberia was an earthly paradise or a hellhole depended on who you talked to. Disappointed would-be settlers forced home by debilitating sickness or financial failure described a land of misery, where even the most determined could never hope to thrive. Others, more fortunate, came back to invest the profits made by successful trading, or to find an American wife to join them in Africa. In Princeton, with its focus on Liberian missionary work, Mary would no doubt have heard many stories during her schooldays—not least because of the legend of brave Cecilia Van Tyne. In Witherspoon Street, Van Tyne's example was a constant reminder of the little community's own links with faraway Liberia. From these tales of returning settlers and missionaries, Mary would have had plenty of time to frame her own imaginative pictures of the new country.

All the same, it was difficult for Mary to get a balanced notion of a place so utterly different from anywhere she'd been before. Up till now, she had spent her whole life in urban environments—in Elizabeth Van Lew's comfortable mansion in the most exclusive part of Richmond, and then in the busy world of Princeton. Both these places were what American people thought of as "civilization." Liberia, on the other hand, was said to be mainly swamps and forests. Now, Mary was about to see for herself.

On Christmas Eve 1855, she left America from New York on the good ship *Lamartine*, for a voyage that was expected to take just over a month. She would not be alone in Liberia, or even on the voyage out—Elizabeth Van Lew had seen to that. She was traveling on the same ship as fifty-five other black emigrants and a white missionary, the Reverend Horne, and his wife. On arrival, she would stay in the family of another married missionary. Her hosts would be expected to look after her (and, no doubt, keep a stern eye on her morals). She would also be under the watchful eye of the Reverend Anthony David Williams, an influential figure in Liberian society. A free emigrant, the former Methodist preacher was a senior politician and one-time agent for the American Colonization Society. In his mid-fifties when Mary arrived in Liberia, he had been in the country for over thirty years. He had recently completed a term of office as Liberia's vice-president under the administration of the country's first president, Joseph J. Roberts.[6]

Even before Mary embarked on the *Lamartine*, Elizabeth had been taking a keen interest in the new country, finding out as much as she could about it from *The African Repository*, the official journal of the Colonization Society. She subscribed to the journal for several months before Mary left America. From its pages she learned about missionary endeavors among the natives, about local customs and beliefs, about how the indigenous people received the American colonists, and how the colonists behaved towards the local people. The journal also gave details on economic development projects: coffee growing, and a new scheme for iron mining; and about the Alexander High School, where boys and young men, the country's future leaders, were being trained in Latin and Greek. The *Repository* published lists of recent emigrants to the new colony, and subscriptions and donations in support of the colonial venture.

Slave-state-based branches of the society, like that in Virginia, tended to be more racist in their motivations for promoting West African settlement. In seeking a role for Mary in Liberia, Elizabeth therefore opted to deal directly with the main Colonization Society in Washington, rather than with any local organization nearer home. As a result, she established useful links with senior ACS members. She made contact with a Baltimore shipping agent, G. W. S. Hall, who would later be elected a "corresponding member" of the ACS Board of Directors, and who handled commissions for emigrants to West Africa. She asked him to send a bag on the steam ship *Mary Caroline*, presumably containing items for Mary in Liberia. In particular, she kept in close touch with the society's secretary-treasurer, the Reverend William McLain, and sometimes approached him with her practical needs. (In April 1857, for instance, she sought his advice on the best way to send a box to Monrovia.)[7]

In October 1854, Elizabeth wrote to thank William McLain for pamphlets he had sent her about Liberia—for materials "pertaining to the good cause in which you are engaged." These, she wrote, "interested me very much," adding, "May God direct and bless you and all who labor with you." Elizabeth was fully convinced that the Colonization Society, by the missionary activity it made possible, was doing the work of God. And now her Mary had been enlisted in that holy work.

Elizabeth was only one among many who saw the hand of God in the Liberia scheme. Another was the Episcopalian missionary Alexander Crummell, who was to become an eminent educator in Liberia. "I believe God has gracious designs for Africa," Crummell wrote in 1861 in *The African Repository*. He regarded Liberia as "one instrument by which He has blessed and will bless Africa."[8] Christians in the nineteenth century were troubled that in whole areas of the globe there existed peoples who did not know that their souls had to be saved, and could only be saved, by faith in Christ. Members of evangelical churches—Presbyterian, Baptist, and Methodist—as well as Episcopalians and Roman Catholics felt it a God-given imperative to win these benighted nations to Christianity. Not surprisingly, although it troubled the missionaries, the natives had never heard of Jesus. "They have no knowledge of the resurrection," one evangelist reported, "and the doctrine is altogether new to them."

The traditional beliefs of the native peoples were particularly shocking to the missionaries. The local people practiced polygamy, worshiped their ancestors, believed in demons and amulets and spirits that lived in trees, and allegedly practiced witchcraft. Some tribes believed in reincarnation. Native funerals involved the burying of grave goods and the pouring of libations into the grave. When someone died, a whole village, both adults and children, might get drunk for days. Particularly troubling for many among the religious colonists was the thought of what awaited the unbaptized in the next life. For their own sakes, these souls must be brought to Jesus.

How strongly young Mary felt any such imperative is impossible to know. True, she had been carefully taught in a pious Christian atmosphere. She had lived for over seven years with the assurance that "When you grow up you will be a missionary." So most probably she shared the conviction of other believers, that the so-called "savages" living in West Africa were lost souls unless dedicated people were willing to go out into the forests and swamplands and teach them how to be saved.

American Presbyterians, who had been so important in Mary's education back in Princeton, were playing a pivotal role in developing missionary and educational work in Liberia. The first Presbyterian church there was established eleven years after the founding of the colony itself. A year later, Presbyterian missionaries began setting out to preach to the natives. By the mid-1800s, Presbyterians counted fifty-nine missionaries in the country out of a total of seventy-five of all denominations. At the University of Liberia, in which Presbyterians also played an important part, they had a key role in training a future generation of Liberian politicians.

Though Liberia was 4,500 miles from New York City, and a hundred more from Mary's birthplace in Virginia, there was all the same a fair amount of coming and going between the mother country and the newly independent former colony. Traders soon began shipping out goods unobtainable in Liberia, and within a few decades were carrying back valuable loads of palm oil and timber to America. Missionaries came back to nurse their health, it having been destroyed by fever or the sultry tropical climate, or to recruit new apostles for the struggle to win souls for Christ. Fresh cohorts of emigrants were constantly setting out in the opposite direction, hoping to start a new life in Africa.

One thing was sure about Liberia: new settlers could not expect to find the comforts of home waiting for them when they arrived. Everything for furnishing a house or following a trade—almost anything that did not actually grow from the West African soil—had to be brought in from America. A pamphlet produced by the American Colonization Society, *Information about Going to Liberia: Things which Every Emigrant to Liberia Ought to Know,* spelled out in detail what would be needed. Settlers were advised to take with them—assuming they could afford such luxuries—their own supply of bedding and "a good mattress." These would be wanted both on the voyage, they were told, and on arrival. A carpenter, or a farmer, must bring along the tools of their trade. All such items were hard-to-get luxuries in Liberia. For setting up house, emigrants had to bring kitchen utensils and "a good supply of table furniture." Hard currency, "some greenbacks, or specie or gold coin," would come in handy too.[9]

Every bit as much as other settlers, Liberia missionaries struggled with the lack of material supplies. In 1844, as one missionary reported apologetically to his superiors back in America, he and his colleagues had not "commenced keeping school on a large plan," because "our provisions will not allow us." In 1850, a Presbyterian living in Monrovia wrote to his sponsors in New York asking them to send not only hymn books, catechisms, and a bell for his church, but even something as basic as writing paper.

Accounts of Liberia by visitors were certainly contradictory. One writer, who introduced himself as "a Colored Clergyman" in a description of Liberia published in 1854, described the country as "more like the Garden of Eden, than any place that I have ever seen or read about." He admired the stone-built churches in Monrovia, the new school there, and what he described as the healthy looks of the people and their livestock.[10] Others might have been writing about a completely different place. One visitor denounced the slum hovels in which poorer emigrants were compelled to live while waiting to be assigned patches of land. Whole extended families, he claimed, were crammed into "leaky huts in which gentlemen in the States would not keep their horses and favorite dogs." William

Nesbit, whose account was published a year after this negative account (and in the year Mary landed at Monrovia), told a similarly gloomy story. Those Colonization Society agents who praised Liberia were, Nesbit claimed, guilty of "most egregious falsehoods." Everything they said was exaggerated. Far from being a paradise, "The whole country presents the most woe begone and hopeless aspect which it is possible for a man to conceive of." He noted the weed-grown streets in the capital, and what he saw as the shabby, weather-beaten look of the buildings. Most of the ordinary houses were not fine mansions or even modest wooden buildings, but "dilapidated frame and bamboo huts." The "meanest village" in the United States, he said, was more attractive than the Liberian capital.

In fact, contrary to Nesbit's testimony, Ashmun Street, the main street of Monrovia, could be a pleasant surprise to an American traveler expecting rows of tumbledown shacks and battered, leaky hovels. There were plenty of these elsewhere in the country—homemade, makeshift dwellings where destitute families with inadequate tools or funds toiled away on the patches of land issued them by the U.S. government. But the main boulevard in Liberia's new capital was lined, by the time of Mary's arrival, with stately clapboard mansions, complete with spacious verandas and whitewashed picket fences that would not have looked out of place in Charleston or the rural outskirts of Richmond. By the mid-1850s, over 2,500 settlers lived in the capital, and there were 8,000 in Liberia altogether.

Not content with criticizing the architecture, however, Nesbit also denounced what he called the "corrupt" administration of President Joseph J. Roberts, Liberia's first elected president. The government was autocratic, Nesbit said, because of the passivity of others in public office. Owing to a lack of education, they preferred to leave everything to be decided by the president. His dishonest dealings, Nesbit claimed, took place "with the support and connivance" of the American Colonization Society.[11]

Others were less harsh in their assessment, calling on the critics to be more realistic and moderate their expectations about conditions in a newly founded colony:

Persons coming to Africa should expect to go through many hardships, such as are common to the first settlement in any new country. I expected it, and was not disappointed or discouraged at any thing I met with; and so far from being dissatisfied with the country, I bless the Lord that ever my lot was cast in this part of the earth. The Lord has blessed me abundantly since my residence in Africa, for which I feel that I can never be sufficiently thankful.

The fertility of the soil "could not be exaggerated," added the ACS pamphlet that published this encouraging statement. Even though there were no plows or oxen in Liberia, and all tilling and plowing had to be done by hand, the profits to be gained from farming there, would, it was claimed, "sweeten the toil." But you still needed the necessary tools. For those with wealth, education, or both—usually people who had been free men and women before they had left America—the land did give hope to start a brand new life. Not surprisingly, it was those who came with nothing—former field slaves and others who arrived destitute—who found life hardest in the new Liberia.

For many, including free blacks living in relative prosperity in Northern cities, the attraction of emigration was freedom. Especially for black Southerners, a new life in Liberia meant escape from the oppressive laws that bound even legally free blacks in fundamental aspects of their lives—aspects such as the denial of the right to vote, and racial segregation in public places. For the Reverend Samuel Williams, after the passing of the Fugitive Slave Act in 1850, whereby an escaped slave could be captured and returned to slavery in the South, the choice of emigration was not difficult: "I wanted a home where I could be free."

For the most educated among black Southerners, intellectual liberty and freedom of worship were often added to the motivations to emigrate. For these people, Liberia meant an end to bans on teaching literacy in churches and to segregated pews in white churches; it meant the lifting of restrictions on the free association of black congregations, and an end to oppressive orders against lingering together to socialize after the service; it meant freedom from whites' surveillance of the preacher's sermon in case it contained anything radical or subversive of white supremacy. One man who yearned to emigrate to Liberia wrote about the prospect of such freedom in lyrical terms:

> In Liberia you can erect a temple to worship God, in the beauty of holiness; without fear you can set up, and protect your sacred altars, and pour out the orisons of the devout and pious heart before them, in praise and thanksgiving to God.

And there would be "no bar" either, the same writer pointed out, to founding places of learning, to instruct the new generation in law, medicine, or theology. "You will there know no superiors but virtue," he believed, "and the laws of your country."[12]

Whatever the pros and cons of life in the new Liberia, for young Mary Richards, it seemed, there was now no turning back. On January 24, 1856, after a journey of five and a half weeks, the *Lamartine* docked at

Monrovia. It was the time of the short dry season, and Mary, with her fellow passengers, disembarked into a hot wind laden with dust blowing from the Sahara.

Every newcomer, rich or poor, and whatever their motives for traveling to Liberia, had to admit that the climate was oppressive. Behind the narrow coastal strip, with its lagoons and swamps a magnet for mosquitoes, the dense forest stretched away out of sight, only penetrable by following the course of inland rivers. The air was nearly always heavy with moisture. From May to October, it rained—and rained. When it was not raining, there were only rare glimpses of the sun, hidden as it was most of the time by thick cloud. In the short dry season from December to late February, the Harmattan wind brought stinging dust swirling through the streets, drifting into houses through open doors and windows, coating shelves and ledges, floors and furniture.

Then there were the diseases—mainly varieties of fever: typhoid, malaria, lassa fever, dengue, yellow fever, along with hepatitis and dysentery. For people without immunity, little knowledge of how an illness like malaria was spread, and little recourse to curative medicines, falling sick was often fatal. In the early years of the colony between 1820 and 1843, out of the first 4,571 emigrants, only 1,819 survived. John Brooke Pinney, the Presbyterian minister who served as acting governor of Liberia before independence, lasted just a few years before being invalided home. For missionaries, even in the 1850s, fever remained an occupational hazard. One has to wonder whether the chronic ill health that would dog Mary Richards throughout her adult life, and sometimes confine her to bed for days at a time, was a result of her time spent in Liberia.

Missionaries often preferred to do their evangelizing work in the relative comfort of Monrovia, teaching the children of former slaves, or attempting, as they saw it, to "civilize" the local African people they employed as servants, and those who came into the town to trade with the settlers. So—particularly given her youth—it is unlikely Mary would have been sent to any of the more distant missionary outposts on the coast, or along one of the rivers that ran from the interior of the country down to the sea. Not that the climate was particularly healthy in Monrovia. Malaria was endemic there, as it was in the rest of the country, spread by mosquitoes that bred in the coastal swamps.

The local food would have been strange to many. It was abundant—there was plenty of fish, game, vegetables, and fruit, along with rice and cassava—but it was rich and spicy, and made some newcomers ill until they got used to it.

It may seem strange to us that a fifteen-year-old should have been expected to teach classes of children not much younger than herself, let alone to talk about Jesus and the Resurrection to strangers in a culture completely different from her own. We have to remember, though, how common such expectations were in the nineteenth century. Thousands of fourteen-year-old boys (and some younger), served on nineteenth-century warships as "powder monkeys," ferrying bags of gunpowder from the ship's store to the guns, or in armies as drummer boys. In schools, it was a common practice in the United States and Britain for gifted older students to act as teachers to younger or less able ones. All the same, it must be admitted that the missionaries who ventured out to Africa and other far-flung places tended to be well out of their teens when they went. Cecilia Van Tyne was twenty-eight when she first traveled to Liberia. When Betsey Stockton sailed for Hawaii, she was already in her early thirties.

Mary was unusual, too, in being given a missionary role in her own right. Although missionaries' wives or sisters often accompanied them to far-flung places, it was normally the men who did the actual preaching and teaching. Even allowing for the cultural traditions of the time, it has to be said that Mary's situation as a Liberian missionary was thus in all respects exceptional. In sending her thousands of miles from home, without the company of former friends or any member of the only family she had ever known, into an environment utterly different from everything familiar to her, Elizabeth was asking a lot of Mary.

There was a crying need in Liberia for teachers for the new emigrants and their families. Many settlers were former plantation slaves who had been denied access to any formal education in America. (Their desire for education was greater, it may be said, than among the indigenous people, who had got along without literacy from time immemorial, and were seemingly none the worse off for it.) If one believed the advice given out by the American Colonization Society, Liberian law required all parents to send their children to school. In practice, though, educational projects were struggling. In 1856, when Mary arrived in the country, only about 1,500 children—mainly the children of settlers—were in school. There was a shortage of books as well as teachers, and only a handful of high schools. The missionary societies in 1857 spent over $90,000 to try and improve the situation—relatively speaking a colossal amount, considering that the entire national governmental budget for that year was just $25,000. If Mary thought about it, her tiny contribution thus made her part of a very significant project.

Given their more sophisticated technology and more complex political structures compared with those of the indigenous Africans, the Liberian settlers thought of themselves as bringing "civilization" to backward peoples. Regarding the indigenous people, the stated aim of one supporting group of the American Colonization Society was as follows:

> To civilize this degenerate people, to change their ignorance into knowledge, their horrible superstition into a right understanding of the Christian Religion, their treachery into good faith, and their sloth into industry.[13]

There were over twenty tribes, speaking twenty different languages. They lived in the dense forest, where they cultivated patches of land for planting by simple slash-and-burn agriculture. They wore next to no clothing, which no doubt helped keep them healthy in the humid climate. Unlike the natives, the settlers went about dressed in what the more prosperous among them would have worn back in America: serge trousers and jackets for the men, with bow ties when formal attire was called for, and long-sleeved dresses for the women that covered them from neck to ankle. Their clothing was part of a newfound pride in their identity as members of a free black republic. To become "civilized," the native peoples were expected to imitate not only the newcomers' religious faith and practices, but also their customs of dress and living.

One thing that could not fail to impress and inspire any black emigrant, old or young, was the new social arrangements. The settlers found themselves in a world where blacks were in power. Wherever Mary went, she saw former slaves and other browbeaten social inferiors standing taller, proudly claiming their new rights, new freedoms, new dignity. She saw black people running the government. Other blacks were traders here; those with capital were able to build up fortunes by dealing in peppers, palm oil, sugar cane, and ivory. Here, emigrants could be homeowners, landowners, respected teachers, and intellectuals. Mary had come from a world where people like herself cowered under the power of the law. Most of the new Liberians had once been literally someone else's property—living under a regime that made them liable to be bought, sold, and subjected to savage punishment if ever they stepped out of line. Here, it was their elected leaders who made the laws and administered them.

Mary would have heard the talk about the greed and dishonesty of many in the government—but was that so different, after all, from the society she had come from? She probably would not have been greatly affected, either, by the settlers' conflicts with the native peoples, which sometimes broke out into open warfare. She might have noticed, however, that native servants working in the emigrants' houses were not always well treated.

On first arriving in Liberia, the poorest settlers themselves, having been given small plots of land along the Mesurado and St. James rivers and left to get on with tilling them and building their own houses, lived in wretched conditions. There was a sharp class division between these struggling farmers and the free blacks who formed the new country's government. But again, this was an issue that probably hardly concerned Mary, living in the relative comfort of a missionary's home.

Daily life in Liberia was, it had to be admitted, generally boring. Anyone able to amuse themselves by playing a musical instrument or by reading or studying was at a certain advantage. The wealthier settlers held balls and concerts, but the most a teenage girl like Mary could expect by way of entertainment was a gathering at the church, or the odd invitation to tea in the house of some minister's wife.

In September, Elizabeth Van Lew wrote to William McLain with unusual urgency. Her letter to him enclosed a second, which she begged him to forward to the Reverend Anthony Williams in Liberia "as soon as possible." Williams, though no longer in the Liberian government, remained an influential figure in Liberian society, and since he had made himself responsible for watching over Mary during her time in the country, Van Lew counted on him to help her. By passing on her letter to Williams, Elizabeth told McLain he would be doing her "a great kindness."

It was, of course, about Mary. She had fallen ill in Liberia. She was miserable there and had written to Elizabeth "imploring and beseeching" her patron to let her come back to America. That was not all, however. Elizabeth learned from Mary's guardians that—for reasons we shall never know—she had upset and angered them. What had she been doing? Had there been teenage tantrums? Screaming? Throwing crockery? Some discreditable escapade?

Whatever the cause, after consulting with her brother John, Elizabeth had decided it would be best for everyone if Mary came home from Liberia. "We think that if anything should happen to her or in case of her death," she wrote, "we should feel very badly on account of keeping her in Africa ... so much against her will.... I am sure the climate does not agree with her, and that may be the reason for her irritability and ill conduct." Among these nineteenth-century puritans, who held propriety and self-restraint in strict regard, it would not be so difficult, after all, for a distressed nineteen-year-old to cause offense—not least if she was partly delirious with some undiagnosed fever.

While Elizabeth was clearly anxious about Mary's illness and unhappiness, she was also deeply embarrassed by her protégée's alleged misbehavior. "That she has conducted herself improperly and given you trouble is a cause of sincere sorrow to us," she wrote to Williams. Whatever it was that Mary was supposed to have done, one senses the strain Elizabeth was under as she struggled to practice Christian forgiveness. "God have mercy upon us," she wrote, "and make and keep us kind and forgiving to one another for Christ's sake." The ever-practical Elizabeth then addressed a few mundane details: "I hope that a bag I sent was safely received—and also twenty five dollars through Mr. McLain...." She went on to discuss how to settle payment of the fare for Mary's journey home: "I do not like to run the risk of sending it." Perhaps she could owe the money, and settle up with whoever paid it, once the ship docked in America?

After addressing these practical issues, she returned to an outpouring of anxious apology, almost as if it was she herself who had somehow misbehaved:

> I do thank you very much for your kindness and care and interest in her—I know that she has been doing very wrong and acting very badly—I will try & do the best I can by her—as I would be done by— May it please God to change her—I think she will be better here.

Concerning Mary herself, her tone was one more of sorrow than anger: "I have written kindly to her—and will not reproach or upbraid her on her return—I will feel less anxiety about her and would rather have her here." After further assurances that the money for Mary's fare would be repaid "immediately upon her arrival," Elizabeth continued to apologize and express her embarrassed thanks—"much gratitude for all your ill-requited trouble."

Normally brisk and business-like in her dealings with the Colonization Society, she let her anxiety break through again, as she asked Williams to understand the intensity of her feelings for Mary:

> I would like [her] to come as soon as possible—I do love the poor creature—she was born a slave in our family—and that has made me always feel an awful responsibility—Oh Mr. Williams how responsible a thing is life!

Elizabeth would pay Mary's passage home. Her guardians in Liberia would advance the money for the fare. Knowing that Mary was ill, Elizabeth asked that she be allowed to travel back in comfort in a cabin, rather than in the crowded steerage, where the poorer passengers all lived crammed in together. (This request was not met, however.)

Early in February 1860, the steamer *Caroline Stevens* sailed away from Monrovia with Mary on board. For her, the Liberian experiment was over. For all the misery it had caused her, Mary's time in Africa would turn out to have had its compensations. For one thing, she had gained a lasting commitment to the teaching profession—not merely as a way of earning a living, but as a vocation. If she could not teach the settlers and natives of Liberia, one day she would use the experience gained to help fellow blacks in America. She had, too—although at the price of the ill health that would drain her all her life—gained a new strength and confidence. She had lived for four years in a strange and difficult environment, forced to rely on her own inner resources. That self-reliance would serve her well in the dangerous challenges that, all unknown to her, still lay ahead.

Little did Mary suspect, as she stepped off the ship's gangplank and set foot once again on American soil, that a dramatic new chapter in her life was about to open.

3

Spies Like Us

*The true history of this war will show that the loyal army found
no friends at the South so faithful, active and daring in their
efforts to sustain the Government as the Negroes.*

—Abolitionist Frederick Douglass

The *Caroline Stevens* docked in Baltimore on March 5, 1860. Mary came back
to live with the Van Lew women—Mrs. Eliza and Miss Bet. She felt the net of
the slave-owning South, with its racist laws, once again cage her in. However
difficult her life in Liberia had been, there she had been a free woman. Before
that, as a child at school in Princeton, she had belonged to a warmly supportive
free black community, where people were valued for themselves and
encouraged to develop their abilities. All that, it seemed, was now over. Here
she was, a gifted young person, trained to teach others, trapped in a world
where, for blacks, any gathering to teach or learn even the most basic literacy
skills was punishable—by fines for whites, and for blacks, by a severe flogging.
Was she then going to be a servant, an over-educated parlor maid in a wealthy
white household, for the rest of her life? What else was there for her to do?

Having been born into slavery in Virginia and then lived in New Jersey
and Liberia, Mary had, in her own words, "breathed the air of freedom."
Now she was suffocating. She was so "nearly in despair," she would later
say of that time in her young life, that she "almost prayed to die."

Richmond had always been a very repressive environment for any black
person. Interracial marriage was banned. Nighttime meetings of slaves
were illegal. Travel was forbidden to slaves, unless the slave had a permit
from the owner. A slave could quite legally be killed during the infliction
of a punishment, without any fear of consequences for the perpetrator.

In the four years Mary had been away, the repression had got worse. The angry debates in Washington, fueled by complaints of Southern landowners about federal taxes on their commerce and by increasingly vocal demands of abolitionists for an end to slavery, were coming to a head. The economic differences between the North and South seemed unresolvable, and likely to lead soon to open conflict. Southerners, growing increasingly insecure and fearful of outright revolts by slaves—despite insisting all the while that slaves were happy in their situation and grateful to their overlords—took draconian measures to keep enslaved people in check. Richmond's new slave code of 1857 banned slaves from hiring themselves out—a long-established custom that had allowed enslaved people to earn a little money to keep for themselves. Slaves were no longer permitted to smoke in public, to carry a stick or cane, to stand on or "obstruct" the sidewalk, to ride in a hackney carriage, or to use "provocative language." Even free blacks could find themselves subject to these petty and draconian laws. All churches with black congregations had to be empty of worshipers thirty minutes after the end of a service. Black people were not allowed to go into certain parts of Richmond, unless they could prove they were there on the orders of their white masters.

Mary's ambiguous legal status now filled her life with uncertainty. Merely by returning to Virginia after her schooling in the North, she was in breach of the law. Under the terms of that law, moreover, she was probably still considered a slave. Although Miss Bet's mother Eliza had assured her slaves they were free, no court ruling had ever officially confirmed that claim. And if Mary *was* legally free, then again, strictly speaking, she had no business to be in Virginia. By a law of 1806, any former slave who remained in the state as a free person for more than a year could—at least theoretically—be arrested and sold back into slavery. (In practice, this particular law was widely disregarded—free blacks living in Richmond contributed substantially to the city's economy, and so were generally left to go about their business.) But a freed slave who had been out of the state and returned—particularly when, like Mary, she was not only literate, but educated beyond a standard considered appropriate for a slave—could never feel wholly safe. The cage of laws designed to control black people and keep them in their place held her in on every side.

Shortly after her return to Richmond, while living in the Van Lew household, Mary went to open the trunk she had brought back from Liberia, and discovered that documents proving her identity were missing. On questioning the Van Lews, she was told they had been removed "for safe-keeping." The papers had been locked away, she learned, so that no one should ever know she been away from Virginia and come back.[1]

To go about in public, all blacks were required to carry a pass—either a "certificate of freedom," or, if a slave, a document issued by the slave owner giving the owner's permission to be walking out alone on some errand. There was a harsh criminal penalty for flouting these Virginia pass laws: a free black person caught without a "certificate of freedom" could be enslaved and sold at public auction.

Mary had been a young child when she had left Virginia for the North. Before then, although enslaved, she had lived a sheltered existence under the protection of the Van Lew family. She had been used to walking in Richmond without hindrance, in the company of a white person or with an older black servant holding her safely by the hand. It is hardly surprising that now, as an independent adult going out of doors by herself, she let her guard drop. On August 20, when she had been back in Virginia less than six months, she ran into trouble.

The Van Lew women would surely have warned Mary against the risks of wandering about Richmond alone, but in August 1860 Elizabeth and her mother were 200 miles away, vacationing at a spa in West Virginia. It was a sultry summer evening, hot and stuffy in the house, and Mary could hardly avoid ever going out on her own. So it was, that walking through the town enjoying the rising evening breeze, she found herself rudely accosted by a watchman who challenged her for her "pass," which she did not have with her.

Mary had a sarcastic tongue. One can well imagine that, when challenged, she answered the watchman back. When she failed to produce the required paper, she found herself under arrest.

This encounter with the naked brutality of the slave system came as a rude shock. It must have been deeply frightening for Mary to find herself arrested and taken to jail. All the same, in an early indication of her ability to think on her feet, which would stand her in good stead in the dangerous years ahead, she kept her wits about her. She gave a false name—two in fact—to different people as she was dragged through the legal system for punishment. She was Mary Jane Henley, she told them. She was Mary Jones.

She would later tell an audience of sympathetic Northerners that on the morning after her arrest she was given five lashes and sold into slavery. It is impossible to verify the truth of this first claim. As to the second, that she was sold into slavery, clearly this never happened. The authorities chose to believe they were dealing with someone who was already a slave, and who had broken the pass law. In a first appearance before the mayor's court, Mary gave a mainly accurate account of herself. According to an account in a local newspaper, *The Richmond Whig*, she told the court that her mother was a slave belonging to Mrs. Van Lew of this city, and that she, the daughter, was sent to the North by Mrs. VL, to be "highly educated", and after receiving her education, was sent to Liberia, from whence she returned, on a visit to this country, a few weeks ago, and came to Richmond at the instance of Miss Van Lew.

Given her Northern education, it would not do to say that she was living in Virginia permanently. She evidently thought it safer to tell the judge that she was merely back from Liberia on a visit. But however she told the story, she was deep in legal hot water. Her ordeal could end with her being sold away to who knew where, possibly to be worked to a premature death on some white owner's plantation.

The *Richmond Whig* reporter found her story suspicious. Something, he realized, did not add up. In his opinion, Liberia, home of freed blacks, was "a strange place" for "a *slave* to go to or come from." Fortunately, the court chose to disbelieve Mary's story about Liberia (mainly true though it was). The charge brought against her applied to a slave caught without a pass, rather than a more serious one of returning to Virginia as a freedwoman with a Northern education. It was lucky, too, that she had connections in Richmond. The Van Lew name was a powerful incentive for the judge to treat her leniently. All the same, she was sentenced to nine days in jail. But it could have been so much worse.

On September 10, Eliza Van Lew was summoned to attend court. Much as if the court had been dealing with a case of strayed cattle, Eliza had to plead guilty to a charge of letting her slave "go at large" without a pass, and pay a $10 fine.

The following year, Mary got married. How it came about is uncertain. Mary's life had come to a dead end and marriage may have seemed to her like a possible way forward. Or possibly the would-be bridegroom took the initiative, taking a liking to Mary and asking Eliza for her hand. Or perhaps it was the Van Lew women who thought marriage could be an antidote to Mary's unhappiness and therefore found someone they deemed suitable for her. The bare fact remains that, according to the parish record in St. John's Church where Mary had been baptized fifteen years before, Wilson Bowser and Mary Richards, "colored servants to Mrs. E. L. Van Lew," were wed. Mary Jane Richards was now Mrs. Mary Bowser.

On April 17, the day after the wedding, Virginia voted to secede from the United States. Mary's connection to Elizabeth was now about to evolve in an unexpected and dangerous direction. She had known "Miss Bet" as a patron, a benefactor, and a domestic employer. With the coming of war, there would soon be a new relationship between them—that of spymaster and spy. To understand how this came about, a digression at this point is called for.

With the rebellion against the Union, the world of the American South stood on the brink of radical change. In 1861, the thing some had dreaded and others longed for, but which grew ever more inevitable, finally happened: one by one, the Southern members of the United States declared their political independence from the North. That could only mean open war. The showdown in April at Fort Sumter, South Carolina, where Southern Confederate troops had succeeded in driving Union forces out, proved to be the catalyst that triggered a devastating military conflict. It was to cost more than 620,000 lives.

Some were exultant at the war's outbreak. Among many in the South, a kind of drunken triumphalism prevailed. Elizabeth Van Lew was an appalled witness of rowdy celebrations in the streets of Richmond:

> That night I went to the bottom of the garden to view the torchlight procession. Such a sight ... the multitude, the mob, the whooping, the tin-pan music, and the fierceness of a surging, swelling revolution ... as the procession passed, I fell upon my knees under the angry heavens, clasped my hands and prayed, "Father, forgive them for they know not what they do!" Mobs went to private houses to hang the true of heart....[2]

Some of those who became the most active supporters of the Southern Confederacy were as dismayed as Elizabeth at the turn of events. Among them was a battle-hardened soldier by the name of Jefferson Davis, soon to be appointed president of the breakaway states. Davis, it was said, was "deeply distressed" by "the temper" of those who unthinkingly celebrated the outbreak of war. "God help us, war is a dreadful calamity even when it is made against aliens and strangers," he was often heard to exclaim. In a haunting echo of Elizabeth Van Lew's words on the thoughtless enthusiasm for the impending carnage, he would quote aloud from the Gospels: "They know not what they do."[3]

Powerless to intervene—but all the same hoping some good for themselves might come out of it all—blacks in the South bided their time, watched, and waited. The more prescient foresaw that a victory for the Union might actually bring about the end of their enslavement. That was by no means guaranteed, however, and they were well aware that this war was less about the monstrous cruelties of slavery than forcing the Southern states to rejoin the Union. President Abraham Lincoln, who would come to be hailed as the great liberator of African Americans, would state emphatically, a year into the war:

If I could save the Union without freeing any slave I would do it, and if I could save it by freeing all the slaves I would do it; and if I could save it by freeing some and leaving others alone, I would also do that.

That the conflict would later be written up as primarily a battle for liberation of the oppressed was a fiction informed by hindsight. Emancipation, if it came, might be a by-product of the war, but not a principal goal. All the same, as many reflected, and Mary Richards Bowser among them, it was a by-product worth fighting for.

Of more immediate significance than U.S. government policy, however, as far as Mary was concerned, were the dramatic changes in the manner of life of her patron Elizabeth. The Van Lew women, mother and daughter, continued to be deeply distressed by the secession of the Southern states. Elizabeth in particular was violently upset. When all was said and done, she and her mother remained deeply attached to their community, their friendships with their neighbors, and the land where they lived. But they were also Americans, with relatives and many friends in the North. Elizabeth in particular was friendly with abolitionists.

At the same time, the Van Lew women had long been ambivalent about declaring outright opposition to slavery. True, they had freed their own slaves; but still, the wealth they continued to enjoy had been generated through slave labor in John Van Lew's hardware stores and on their farmland near Richmond. And they numbered many slave owners among their friends. Whatever private arrangements the women might have made to ease their consciences, to have openly declared themselves in favor of universal abolition would have made them pariahs in their own community.

Elizabeth had for many years favored only the gradual emancipation of slaves. She chose to believe that "slave power" was "losing strength before the increasing influence of honest and enlightened free labor," and that over time, waged labor would prove economically more efficient and gradually replace unpaid servitude. For a long time, she clung to this comforting doctrine—even though the conditions under which so many slaves suffered and died, working to the end of their lives without hope of release, grieved her deeply. But she would not challenge the system publicly, only supporting her mother's choice to free the Van Lew slaves, and calling on her friends and neighbors to treat those in their power with humanity.

The coming of the war, however, changed everything for her. She became an out-and-out abolitionist: "This heavy heart pulsing and looking upon Slavery as it really is.... No pen, no book, no time can do justice to the wrongs it honors." Van Lew had come to believe that the institution, cruel as it was to the enslaved, also demoralized and corrupted the slaveholder. She denounced a system that, she believed, "takes away a man's moral or highest courage and replaces it with ... brute valor." Power based on slavery was, she wrote, "despotic—not only over the slave, but over the community."

Elizabeth also became devoted to the Union cause—to having the South rejoin the United States. The founding of the Confederacy seemed to her a kind of madness. Hearing of the outbreak of fighting in Baltimore, and the routing of Union troops there, she could "scarcely see or work," she wrote in her journal, for her "bitter, blinding" tears: "My country! Oh, my country!" But she would not succumb helplessly to grief. Having seen the Confederate flag raised over the Virginia State Capitol in Richmond, she could not recall ever having experienced "a feeling of more calm determination and high resolve for endurance over me, than at that moment."[4]

Elizabeth's active treachery—if one can call it that—to the Confederate cause was first motivated by her distress at the suffering of captured Union soldiers struggling for life, filthy and neglected in Richmond's hospitals, or held in appalling conditions in the prisons. From childhood, she had heard family stories of her aunt Letitia, who had helped relieve the suffering of prisoners of the British during the American Revolution. Now she would do the same for the surviving casualties of the Civil War.

Libby Prison was a former food warehouse on Tobacco Row, situated on the James River waterfront. For Elizabeth, it would have been no more than a fifteen-minute walk from her home. She got permission to visit the prison, and later the war wounded in the hospitals, taking in clean undergarments, food, bandages, and medicine for the Union soldiers. These compassionate visits did not make her popular with her fellow Richmonders, who often viewed them as acts of disloyalty to the Confederate cause: "The threats, the scowls, the frowns of an infuriated community; who can write of them? I have had brave men shake their fingers in my face and say terrible things...."[5]

She quickly learned to aid the Union cause in more clandestine ways. It was not long before she crossed the line from humanitarian aid into gathering intelligence from the captured men. As they arrived from the battlefront where they had been taken prisoner, they had many tales to tell—of Confederate troop movements, of the state of rebel fortifications, of the morale of certain military units.

In her charitable visiting, Elizabeth sometimes took Mary with her. Together, they carried coded messages in and out of the prisons and hospitals, hidden in the lower compartment of a double-bottomed custard dish, its upper compartment filled with soup or custard.

Mary was involved in, or at least aware of, some of Elizabeth's other early wartime activities. She knew of secret nightly meetings at the Van Lew house on Church Hill—"a certain beautiful white dwelling," where, as Mary recalled, "a few faithful ones used to meet night after night" to exchange information for passing on to the Union commanders. How much she was directly involved in these meetings we will never know. It is clear, though, that Elizabeth Van Lew had already come to regard her protégée as a trusted ally in her work for the Union cause.

Other Van Lew domestic servants and farm workers came to play important roles in Elizabeth's network—principally as couriers. Members of the Roane family—William, Peter, and James—and a man named Oliver Lewis tramped the roads north with coded messages hidden in a piece of sewing, in a basket of eggs, under a loose flap inside the sole of a shoe, or scribbled in the margins of a book like a shorthand annotation. These courageous people worked a relay system from one safe house to another, till the message reached the Union lines. They fed vital information to the generals fighting to force the rebel Southern states back into the Union.

It was not long before Elizabeth was contacted by Benjamin Butler, a Union general and commander of what would become known as the Army of the James. He enlisted her, unpaid, to work for the Union on a regular basis. He offered her a code to use in conveying her messages, but Elizabeth preferred to use her own.

Intelligence gathering on both sides of the conflict in the Civil War was a hit-and-miss affair. The Union, benefiting as it did from federal government oversight, had a Bureau of Military Information, which supplied information directly to commanders in the field. It would come to rely on the services of Alan Pinkerton and his newly founded Union Intelligence Service. (Incidentally, it was the first such agency to employ a black detective, John Scobell.) Or self-recruited agents like Elizabeth Van Lew might opt, or be co-opted, to communicate directly with a particular general, as Elizabeth did with General Butler and later with Ulysses S. Grant, bypassing the bureaucratic delays and confusion that could occur where information was first submitted to a centralized government agency.

As a member of Richmond's elite, Elizabeth knew people in many different walks of life. It was remarkable, she discovered, how many sympathizers she could rely on. She herself went out sometimes on clandestine errands as a courier, wearing a large calico bonnet and gaiters, and carrying a countrywoman's basket. Even so, she was concerned that others might recognize her. Her cousin Anna Whitlock recalled how she changed her appearance in order not to be spotted, padding out her cheeks with cotton to fatten her face. Friends claimed that she sometimes adopted an absent-minded manner in public—singing little songs, muttering under her breath, and gazing intently with a vacant smile at people she came across. If she ever did so, it would have been to deflect hostility—to project the unspoken message, "I am eccentric but harmless." All the same, after the war had ended, many of Elizabeth's enemies labeled her with the slur "Crazy Bet." In her dealings with high-ranking government officials, however, and others whose support she needed, her manner would have been that of a dignified, respectable, upper-class member of the community.

Elizabeth's clandestine operations soon developed into helping imprisoned Union soldiers to escape from captivity and find their way back to the North. For this purpose, she used a concealed room at the back of an attic in her family's mansion at Church Hill. It was a hiding place that had previously served a similar use in America's Revolutionary War. Here, the escaped men stayed until arrangements could be made for safe passage back to their units.

In February 1864, there was a dramatic mass breakout from Libby Prison through a tunnel dug by the Union prisoners. By this time, the Confederate authorities in Richmond had come to suspect that the Van Lews were sheltering escaped Union soldiers. Mary would later tell—without mentioning any names or the location of the safe house—of a visit to the Van Lew mansion by Confederate agents posing as escaped Unionists. Pretending to need help, the men said they had heard the occupants of the house gave aid to Union fugitives. "No, no," said "the lady of the house," according to Mary. "No Unionists here."[6]

If the townsfolk were suspicious and resentful when they learned of Elizabeth's errands of mercy to the Union prisoners, they would have been openly hostile and vengeful had they known that, from their opulent home in the select neighborhood of Church Hill, Elizabeth and her servants ran an underground railroad to the North.

By the end of the conflict in 1865, Elizabeth Van Lew's intelligence system linked her not only to the Union military, but to most of the important Confederate offices in Richmond. What the Union generals came to dub "the Richmond Ring" had spies in the departments of the Confederate army and navy, in the post office, and on the railways. Elizabeth had a gift for selecting a capable person for a given task, and for knowing how to delegate risky responsibilities to those she trusted. Also—remarkably for a Southern lady in a patriarchal society, where upper-class women were expected to occupy mainly ornamental roles—she was able to inspire confidence in the men who worked under her direction. She could rely on the skill and courage of people as dedicated to the cause of the Union and the ending of slavery as she was herself; and not only her own servants, who took food and clothing to the Union prisoners and risked their lives in so many dangerous ways, but others, too, from diverse backgrounds. The agents whose work she coordinated included farmers and household slaves, clerks in the Confederate military, machinists, seamstresses, tradesmen, and disaffected private soldiers. We know the names of a few of these people—William Fay, Elias Nuckols, Lemuel Babcock, William Rowley, Thomas McNiven, and Mary Richards Bowser.

Van Lew even had an agent in Libby Prison. The prison clerk, Erasmus Ross, made a point of making himself hated by the Union prisoners for his harsh manner, swearing at and insulting them; calling them "yellow-bellied Yankees." It was all a cover for his Union sympathies. On one famous occasion, he summoned a frightened prisoner to his office, where he silently pointed the man to a back room. In it, the Union soldier found a Confederate uniform. The grateful man put on the disguise and made his escape to the street outside, where he found an agent of Van Lew's waiting to guide him to her house on Church Hill. (Elizabeth regularly employed a number of such trustworthy men to hang around Libby Prison, on the lookout for any Union prisoner making his escape and in need of an escort to safety.)

Poor whites, and black people like Mary more than anyone, ran the greatest risks in their missions. For the latter especially, the automatic consequence of discovery would have been torture and death. Van Lew's servant William Roane was arrested in the street and accused of belonging to the spy ring. It is not known precisely what became of him, but he was never seen again.[7] However committed these black agents might have been to the cause of a Union victory and an end to slavery, it is an indication both of their commitment to the cause and their trust in Van Lew that they carried out their dangerous missions so faithfully.

Any organizer, regardless of the particular enterprise, earns respect and wins the confidence of others by leading from the front. Van Lew did not ask others to do anything she was not prepared to do herself. She shared the tasks, and the risks. She herself visited the prisons, carried hidden messages in her custard dish, took care of the escapees hidden in her attic, or in her farm woman's disguise walked along the roads northwards at dusk, carrying encoded information towards its destination.

On one occasion, she took a serious personal risk to recruit a new agent. When a message from General Butler inviting a certain Confederate officer to defect to the Union side was put into her hands, Van Lew took it to the man herself. From the point of view of the Confederacy, it was an incitement to treason. She watched the officer as he read Butler's letter:

She had sounded him, had found him dissatisfied, approachable....
Against her estimate of character she had staked her life; was she to

win or lose? In the next room were the detectives and armed guards, the machinery of the Confederate capital's secret police; X had but to raise his voice.... She saw his face blanch and his lips quiver; as he followed her out he begged her to be prudent—if she would never come there again he promised to go to her.[8]

Such boldness, though, was exceptional. Another factor in the trust Elizabeth inspired is the extreme caution with which she normally operated—not least when the security of others was at stake. "We have to be watchful and circumspect," she reminded herself in a journal entry in June 1862. "Wise as serpents and harmless as doves," she quoted from the Gospels, "for truly lions are seeking to devour us."[9]

She had many ingenious devices. She used the ornamental lions either side of her living-room fireplace as a post box for others in her house to pick up messages without having to contact her directly. She slept at night with the key to her coded messages tucked away in the back of a watch she kept with her always, along with any compromising paperwork, so that if need arose she could quickly destroy it. She had a grave responsibility, not only to her mother who was now elderly, frail, and ill, but to all those who put their liberty and lives in her hands. She kept a journal but burned much of its contents immediately after writing. The rest, she would keep safely buried until after the war. Even in the postwar years, although she became an outspoken advocate for the education of former slaves, she hardly spoke about her undercover work—aware that others more vulnerable to reprisals than herself could still be put at risk.

Sometimes, Elizabeth achieved her ends by deploying her social skills. She charmed Richmond's military governor, Provost Marshal John Winder, with flattery, even complimenting him on his beautiful silvery white hair. She was adept at pitting one official against another. Blocked for a time from visiting wounded Unionist prisoners, she went over the hospital administrator's head to appeal to the Confederate treasury secretary, Christopher Memminger. When Memminger hesitated to restore her right to visit—the enemy soldiers, he said, were rogues and hooligans, who did not deserve such attention—she congratulated him on a speech she had heard him make at a religious convention. True Christianity must, she was sure he would agree, "begin with charity to the thankless." Memminger granted her request. And when she needed the support of Albert Bledsoe, assistant secretary of war and yet another challenger of her right to deliver custard to sick prisoners, she took him a sample of the custard.

She had always to be on her guard against entrapment. Once, as she was walking along a road towards the Union lines, carrying information about the state of Richmond's defenses, a stranger in civilian clothes caught up with her. "I'm going through the lines tonight," he told her—an implicit invitation to entrust him with some mission. Just as she was about to confide in him and ask him to carry her message to General Ulysses S. Grant, some warning instinct stopped her. The following day, she saw the man again. He was in Confederate uniform, marching to the front with his unit.[10]

As part of her cover for her rescue and spying activities, Elizabeth even took the drastic action of inviting one of the prison commandants, Captain George Gibb, and his family to live in her home. She and her mother were both careful to be seen from time to time helping Confederate soldiers, as well as Union prisoners, with money and material goods. (Elizabeth was happy to aid Confederate private soldiers, who were mostly hapless conscripts from poor families. It was the elite and wealthy she blamed for the South's rebellion and the subsequent terrible war.)

Van Lew's sense of duty to a cause went hand in hand with her driven personality—she could not rest until she had done her utmost to make herself of use, both to the Union cause and to the individuals she comforted and saved. She tirelessly lobbied officials, cared for the fugitives hidden in her attic room, encoded and decoded messages, networked with a growing team of dedicated agents, and visited sick and wounded prisoners. For four long years, these activities consumed every moment of her waking life.

The disloyal opinions of Elizabeth and her mother, publicly expressed before the war—even as voiced within their home, and on one occasion reported to the authorities by Elizabeth's sister-in-law, Mary Van Lew—could in themselves have led to their imprisonment and the confiscation of all their property, followed by deportation to the North. But Elizabeth enjoyed powerful protection. One element that kept her safe was undoubtedly her social position and its effect on others' perceptions of her. Her wealth, too, protected her—not least through her ability to bribe officials into looking the other way when her loyalty to the Confederacy might otherwise have been questioned. It had also gained her access into unlikely places, including military prisons.

Other social stereotypes came into play. The Van Lew family had always had an unimpeachable reputation for honest dealing (as understood within the context of a slave-holding society). The Van Lew women—Eliza and Elizabeth in particular—were known for their charitable generosity and their kindness to the less fortunate. Despite their controversial views, they were Southern ladies, reared in a genteel atmosphere, with behavior assumed to be above reproach. Who would dare directly accuse Eliza or her daughter of doing anything underhand? Besides, Confederate propaganda sought to portray Southerners as more civilized than the allegedly barbaric foe they were fighting. To mistreat an upper-class Southern lady would call that myth into question. Mary Richards Bowser, Elizabeth's faithful acolyte, would not enjoy the same protection if caught.

Elizabeth was a consummate organizer. She would have made a good general, and in a way, she was one. She knew how to choose people for particular roles, matching tasks with capabilities, and to assess whom she could safely trust. In her judgment of character, she seldom made a mistake. She also had a gift for strategy, deploying her agents wherever she found they could be most useful. If there was a negative side to these traits, it was that she tended at times to treat other people as instruments of her purpose. One of those instruments—if clearly a willing one—was her protégée, Mary Richards Bowser.

Mary had quickly become a useful and dependable part of Elizabeth's network, working beside her patron from the earliest days of the war. As we have seen, she was privy to a great deal that went on at the Church Hill mansion, from the clandestine meetings of fellow agents to the concealment of escaped prisoners in the hidden room in the attic.

In August 1861, a new spying opportunity presented itself. Jefferson Davis, now president of the Confederacy, had just moved his government and family to Richmond and settled there in a new home. To Elizabeth, it must have seemed too good a chance to miss. She had a daring idea, but it required a person with a clear head and a cool nerve; it would place them in significant danger. She put her idea to Mary Richards Bowser.

Jeff, Varina—and "Little Mary"

The chief source of information to the enemy is through our
negroes. They are easily deceived by proper caution.

—Robert E. Lee, in a letter to a subordinate[1]

In the course of the war, this piece of wishful thinking on the part of
Confederate General Lee would be severely tested. One of those who
would give the lie to Lee's belief that black people's active support to the
enemy could easily be outwitted by proper attention to security, was a new
servant to President Jefferson Davis.

There was much excitement among Richmonders when Davis brought
his government and family to town, allocating his cabinet members to
offices in the Virginia customs building on the north side of Main Street.
He and Mrs. Davis were soon established in a handsome gray-stuccoed
neoclassical mansion on East Clay Street, in the affluent Shockoe Hill
neighborhood. When the new Confederate president first installed his
family there, it was known simply as the Brockenbrough Mansion after
the first owner, wealthy banker John Brockenbrough. It only later came
to be known as the White House of the Confederacy. The house was
conveniently located a few hundred yards away from the former Custom
House, where Confederate cabinet members had their offices.

Jefferson and Varina had brought two favorite slaves with them from
their plantation in Mississippi, but they required a much bigger staff to
run the new house and entertain in a style befitting their political and
social roles. Most of their slaves and servants were therefore hired locally,
in Richmond. The "upper" servants were free white men and women from

European backgrounds. Edward Eggeling, the German-American who had designed the original gardens of the house for the Brockenbrough family, became the Davises' steward, responsible for the overall management of the household, including finances and the hiring of most of the staff. Personally chosen by Varina were the Irish housekeeper, Mary O'Melia, and an Irish nanny named Catherine. (This nanny was either to give notice, or was sacked, after the tragic death of Joseph Evan, the Davises' five-year-old son.) Among the black enslaved employees were a coachman, William Jackson, Varina's personal maid Betsey, and Jefferson Davis's manservant Robert Brown. And then there was Mary.

We should not be surprised that the Davises took Mary into their household. It was a common practice in Richmond at the time for slave owners to hire out their slaves as a source of income for the master or mistress. Sometimes (not always), the slave also would be paid a tiny percentage of the hire fee, but the main payment went to the slave owner doing the hiring out. (As we have seen, the Van Lews' temporary cook Caroline had worked in their home on just such a basis.)

There are two versions of how Elizabeth managed to install Mary as a member of the Davis household. According to one legend, it was she herself who, on a visit to the Davises' home, observed the clumsiness of Varina's servants as they waited on the guests at table, and recommended Mary.[2] More probably, though, Elizabeth would have stayed out of sight and enlisted a go-between—an agent or a friend—to make the approach and get Mary accepted into the White House of the Confederacy. In this more likely scenario, neither the Davises nor their staff would have been aware that this new "slave" brought into their employment had been sent by Elizabeth Van Lew.

However it came about, the deal was quickly done. Elizabeth now had an agent installed in the Davis family home, the rebel president's de facto headquarters, and the very heart of the Confederacy.

Jefferson Davis, Mary's new master, had the reputation of a benevolent owner. Slaves on the Davis Brierfield plantation in Mississippi were not whipped or beaten, and were well fed and clothed. Elizabeth could be fairly confident that Mary would at least not be physically abused during her time in the president's household, however long it might last. One former slave who ran away from the house to the North before the war ended would, it is true, say that Jefferson's wife Varina was "a devil" to work for. Davis himself, though, as many testified who knew him well, had a kindly, if patronizing, attitude to those he considered his inferiors. According to Varina:

He never had with soldiers, children or negroes any difficulty to impress himself upon their hearts. In his intercourse with them he always assumed that they were reasonable beings, able and willing to follow a proper line of conduct, and capable of understanding mistakes when pointed out to them. Blind obedience was never exacted ... he carefully explained the reasons for doing or not doing a thing and was not satisfied until the understanding was complete.

Varina's husband was, as she said, "abnormally sensitive" to others' disapproval, in a way that made him stiff and ill at ease with anyone he felt to be his equal or superior. "Even a child's disapproval discomposed him," Varina said. "He felt how much he was misunderstood, and the sense of mortification and injustice gave him a repellent manner." Emotionally insecure in his dealings with social equals, he felt comfortable in conversation with slaves, much as he did with children—offering similar condescension to both. Davis prided himself that, unlike many other slave owners, he was not personally brutal. If anything, he enjoyed the slaves' company. He believed he understood them, and that they genuinely liked him—as, at times, some of them possibly did.[3]

In common with many other masters who liked to view themselves as benevolent to those they held in bondage, the Davises had an implicit faith in the loyalty of their slaves. Varina's friend Mary Chesnut, a frequent visitor to the Davises' Richmond home, knew better.

Mary was, like Jefferson Davis, a member of the slave-owning Southern elite. Her husband James, a lawyer, would become a Confederate officer during the Civil War. Her father, a former governor of South Carolina, had, like his son-in-law, served as a U.S. senator. After buying up land in Mississippi, he came to own three plantations, worked by hundreds of slaves. Chesnut had thus grown up in a world where slave owning by the ruling class was the social norm. But, unlike many others of her class, she had a shrewd idea that the stability of her world could not be taken for granted. During the first battle of the Civil War, when the shelling of Fort Sumter could be clearly heard only miles from the porch of her South Carolina home, and people were speculating about a possible Union victory, it occurred to Chesnut to wonder what was going on in the heads of her slaves:

Not by one word or look can we detect any change in the demeanor of these negro servants. Lawrence sits at our door, sleepy and respectful and profoundly indifferent. So are they all, but they carry it too far. You could not tell that they even heard the awful roar going on in the bay, though it has been dinning in their ears night and day. People talk before them as if they were chairs and tables. They make no sign. Are they stolidly stupid? Or wiser than we are; silent and strong, biding their time?[4]

How would Chesnut have reacted if she had known about that other unnoticed "slave" working quietly about the Confederate president's house, taking careful note of everything around her?

It seems unlikely that Jefferson Davis ever asked himself the kind of questions that preoccupied Mary Chesnut. He was a devout Christian, who tried to live by the maxim of "Do as you would be done by," and was generous and charitable to those in need. However, he repeatedly defended the institution of slavery with a breathtaking sense of entitlement and superiority:

> By the existence of negro slavery, the white man is raised to the dignity of a freeman and an equal. Nowhere else will you find every white man superior to menial service.... Your own menial who Blacks your boots, drives your carriage, who wears your livery, and is your own in every sense of the word, is not your equal; and such is society wherever negro slavery is not the substratum on which the white race is elevated to its true dignity.

Slavery, Davis argued further, was essential to the war effort. Victory in the war, he believed, actually depended on "the much-abused institution" of "African servitude," for it enabled "white men to go into the army, and leave the cultivation of their fields and the care of their flocks, as well as of their wives and children, to those who ... were 'held to service or labor.'"

People of African descent were naturally inferior, Davis believed, and their inferiority a condition "stamped upon that race of men by the Creator." It followed, therefore—conveniently enough—that blacks needed to be kept in check under the tutelage of a "superior" race. The slave system, he wrote, was "nothing but the form of civil government instituted for a class of people not fit to govern themselves." It was "just that kind of control which is extended in every northern State over its convicts, its lunatics, its minors, its apprentices." According to Davis's logic, if left to their own devices, without the protective care of benevolent owners, black people would commit crimes and end up "in penitentiaries and workhouses."[5]

Mary Richards Bowser probably never heard, or read a report, of these exact words of Davis, spoken before the war in the U.S. Senate when a senator from Mississippi. But she must surely have heard similar sentiments expressed by other whites. She knew her people would have to fight with every means at their disposal if they hoped to win freedom and equality in America. The chronic racism of white Southerners made her all the more determined to play a part in bringing an end to the cruel system that men like Davis attempted to justify.[6]

In other attitudes and political opinions, the new president was, in many respects, a mass of contradictions. Devotedly loyal to the South where he had grown up, as a Mississippi senator in Washington he had done everything in his power to resist the withdrawal of the Southern states from the Union. In January 1861, he had supported a proposed peace initiative "in the interests of harmony and pacification." As a military veteran of the Mexican–American campaign of 1846–48, who had personally witnessed the carnage of the battlefield, he was deeply concerned about the suffering that would come with the outbreak of civil war. He condemned the enthusiasm on both sides in the Senate for "the prospect of the conflict," which was to "drench the land with blood and enshroud thousands of homes in mourning."[7] As the war dragged on through four long years and the toll on human life grew greater and greater, he repeated these sentiments, Varina said, with "glistening eyes and faltering voice." And yet, a soldier at his core, once war had been declared, he had been eager to be given command of the Confederate military:

> I thought myself better adapted to command in the field, and Mississippi had given me the position which I preferred to any other—the highest rank in her army. [He had at that time been appointed major-general of the state forces.] It was, therefore, that I afterward said ... that the duty to which I was thus called was temporary, and that I expected soon to be with the Army of Mississippi again.

He was quietly pottering about in his garden at Brierfield when the telegram arrived to tell him of his appointment as Confederate president. Varina watched her husband closely as he read, recalling later that "when reading the telegram he looked so grieved that I feared some evil had befallen our family. After a few minutes' painful silence he told me, as a man might speak of a sentence of death."

She witnessed his swearing in at the Virginia State Capitol in February 1862: "As he stood pale and emaciated, dedicating himself to the service of the Confederacy, evidently forgetful of everything but his sacred oath, he seemed a willing victim going to his funeral pyre." It was, Varina said, "his martyrdom."[8] Thus, reluctantly, having performed well in his role as U.S. secretary of war in the Franklin Pierce administration—reforming the army, improving pay and conditions for ordinary soldiers, and overseeing major civil works and infrastructure projects—he was appointed to the rebel presidency. He accepted his election as a matter of duty, and would carry out the unwelcome task to the bitter end, feeling all the while that he was in the wrong job.

Whether suited to the task or not, President Davis had a war to run, and hence no time to oversee the conduct of his household. In any case, that work traditionally fell to a man's wife or other close female relative. Varina, however, was only nominally in charge of domestic affairs, and preferred to leave much of that work to others. She delegated the day-to-day running of the house to Eggeling and to the housekeeper, Mary O'Melia. If Mary Richards Bowser was to win acceptance in the Davis household and carry on working there in her role as a hired-out slave, it was first and foremost Mary O'Melia whom she had to please. Of course, she could not afford to upset Mrs. Davis either, but it is possible that Varina, with her busy social life, intellectual interests, and charitable causes, hardly noticed the new maid.

Over a dozen servants and slaves served in the Davis household at any one time, and some twenty individuals worked there during the four years of the war. There was hiring of new personnel, and firing of those found unsuitable, and there were call-ups of slaves for service to the military, to fetch and carry, or to work on building barricades. As we shall see, a few servants, including the enslaved ones, simply walked out. No records were kept of staff members, their hours, their wages, or even in some cases their names. As for Mary, she would have been using a pseudonym. We do not know what name she used. Either "Richards" or "Bowser" would have led back to those known opponents of secession, Mrs. and Miss Van Lew, so probably she went under a new name altogether. She would also very likely have feigned illiteracy; so that when Varina, in a newspaper interview in 1905, denied all knowledge of an educated female slave working in her house during the Civil War, she may have been telling the truth.

When Varina Howell married Jefferson Davis—his first wife having died of fever in 1835, only three months into their marriage—he was thirty-six and she just eighteen. She found him romantic and fascinating—his lean features, his military bearing, his intense blue eyes, and his air of confidence in his own views and decisions. Later on in their marriage, and particularly where his conduct of the war was concerned, she would begin to doubt his infallibility.

During the war, and in the years that followed, Davis would be criticized by his enemies—and even by some of his friends—for his tendency to appoint his favorites to Cabinet and military posts, for his overly cautious and hesitant approach to decision-making, for his almost neurotic obsession with minute details, and for his insistence on trying to micro-manage every aspect of Confederate military campaigns, where decisions should have been delegated to the commanders in the field. Varina, however, knew better than to argue with her husband or to presume to know about matters of military strategy. She held her tongue and tended to her own interests and the needs of her family.

Varina would bear her husband five children in all, only one of whom would outlive her parents—their daughter Varina Anne, born in the Richmond mansion in 1864. When Varina and Jefferson arrived in Richmond, they had three sons with them—Jefferson Davis Jr., Joseph Evan, and William—and a daughter, Margaret. Varina had also fostered a mixed-race child, Jim Limber, whom she had rescued from the street when she had witnessed him receiving a savage beating from his guardian. Regarded as a sort of household pet by the adults, Jim became a friend and companion to the children. All the children were indulged by both parents, and pretty much allowed to run wild—"wonderfully clever and precocious ... with unbroken wills," Varina's friend Mary Chesnut said of them.[9] The wild brood sowed chaos in the house, making plenty of extra work for the harassed and exhausted servants.

At times—as in her rescue of Jim Limber—Varina showed herself capable of compassion and kindness. She gave presents to orphans at Christmas. She gave money to help the wounded in Richmond's hospitals. Like her husband, though—indeed, like the majority of Southerners—she defended the institution of slavery on which the prosperity of the Southern states relied. It was a subject on which she was wholly incapable of objectivity.

If Varina deferred to her husband's views and wishes over most issues, that deference did not disguise a forceful personality. Even the role she adopted of compliant wife was born of an effort of will. In photographs, her eyes have a steady, penetrating gaze that suggest she was nobody's fool and that she did not tolerate foolishness in others. She was known for her witty repartee, her sarcasm, and her intellectual curiosity. She was well read in contemporary literature and romantic poetry, and given to making literary allusions and throwing out quotations to make an ironic point. None of this endeared her to the ladies of Richmond, among whom intellectual attainments were not encouraged. Erudition and cleverness were thought superfluous in a gentlewoman—even unladylike. (One Richmond lady, it is said, was proud to boast that she had never read a book in her whole adult life.)

Even Varina's looks—her dark eyes and hair—were wrong for Southern society. Her forthright manner, too, made her something of a misfit in a town where ladies were admired for their decorative appeal—for blonde prettiness and graceful manners. And there was racist speculation about the origin of her olive complexion. That, and her small height, led spiteful people to nickname her "The Squaw." It is hardly surprising that Varina's first experience of polite Richmond society was one of "offishness," as she termed it, with a "wary welcome" from the ladies.

It did not help that the Davises did not give the large public "open house" dinners that were expected of them as the Confederate first family. As Varina explained:

Habituated as we were to giving numerous entertainments of an official character, we should gladly have kept up the custom; but during every entertainment, without exception, either the death of a relation was announced to a guest, or a disaster to the Confederacy was telegraphed to the President. He was a nervous dyspeptic by habit, and if he was forced to eat under any excitement, was ill after it for days. He said he could do either one duty or the other—give entertainments or administer the Government—and he fancied he was expected to perform the latter service in preference; and so we ceased to entertain, except at formal receptions or informal dinners and breakfasts given to as many as Mr. Davis's health permitted us to invite. In the evening he was too exhausted to receive informal visitors.

The local press was not sympathetic, and denounced what it called "the parsimony" of the new Confederate administration.[10]

Varina attracted suspicion, too, on account of her Northern family connections. Her descent on her mother's side from a family of wealthy plantation owners in Natchez, Mississippi, never quite compensated, in Southerners' eyes, for the fact that her grandfather had been governor of New Jersey and that she had cousins in the North. Her Union sympathies— at least on a humanitarian level—led her to pay visits to wounded Union prisoners of war, taking them medicine and food. She kept these errands a close secret—from her husband, as well as everyone else—but she still ran a considerable risk of exposure and consequent scandal. She must sometimes have longed to be back in Washington as a senator's wife, mingling with other representatives' wives from all over the United States, and with those whom she could feel were her intellectual equals.

Of more concern to Mary Richards Bowser, however, was what kind of a mistress Mrs. Davis was, and how she treated those who were dependent upon her goodwill. Whether or not we take the coachman William Jackson's word that she was "a devil" to work for, what we know of her fastidiousness and capacity for sarcasm suggests she could be an exacting mistress who wanted everything in her home to be done "just so."

Varina liked the new house assigned to her family by the Richmond City administration. Since the place had been built in 1818, successive occupants had enlarged and improved it, adding a bathroom on the first floor and building a new floor above. The bathroom had running water and the rooms were lighted by gas. Varina was particularly pleased with the garden, with its hillside terraces planted with apple and cherry trees. For a house of its size, the rooms were relatively few, but as Varina remarked, they were spacious.

She had good taste. The dining room and the adjoining reception rooms were relatively uncluttered with knick-knacks, compared with most contemporary homes of the wealthy.

In the crimson-decked salon, where large groups of guests were entertained, the walls were decorated with lively hunting scenes and Confederate flags. Also on display were samples of handmade objects crafted and presented as gifts by Southern soldiers freed from imprisonment in the North in prisoner exchanges. A small adjoining room, referred to by the family as "the snug," could be closed off for a tête-à-tête with a friend, or connecting doors could be opened wide to make it part of the main salon.

This ground floor, where Mary and the other upstairs servants were kept busy waiting on the Davises and their guests, had an elegant dining room with green brocaded sofas and gracefully carved upright chairs. It was reserved for special family occasions, for dinner parties, and for councils of war. (At other times the Davises had their meals in a room in the basement. The servants would have eaten at a table in the adjoining kitchen, after the family had been served.) In the "state dining room," as Varina called it, cabinet members and Confederate generals met for intense, lengthy discussions on administrative policy and military strategy. The oval mahogany table in the center of the room sometimes glittered with plate and fine china, and at others, writing materials were arranged on the bare polished wood in preparation for a meeting of civilian leaders or military officers. From 1863 onwards, a bust of the revered Confederate general, Thomas "Stonewall" Jackson, modeled from the deceased hero's death mask, gazed out from a shelf at the living.

The way up from the more public reception rooms to the private family apartments was, at least for the family and their guests, by a winding spiral staircase. (The servants would have used a different, but equally arduous, set of stairs.) The topmost floor was given over to guest bedrooms and the living quarters of the more important servants. In the Davises' bedroom on the floor below, Jefferson and Varina shared a double bed—unusually for the customs of the time, where well-to-do married couples normally slept in separate rooms. Varina had her own separate smaller space next door—a dressing room-cum-study, where she read, wrote, and sewed within easy reach of her children playing or sleeping in the nursery nearby.

The president's private office, also conveniently close to the couple's bedroom, could be accessed only by going through an antechamber, where those privileged visitors allowed to come upstairs could wait until he was ready to see them. During the daytime, this outer room was guarded by Burton Harrison, Davis's faithful secretary.

In the gardens outside the mansion were outbuildings, where some of the slaves and servants spent their short nights before getting up to begin their sixteen-hour work days. Not all of them slept there, however. A hired-out servant, even if a slave, might go back to his or her master or mistress at night, or possibly even be permitted to sleep in lodgings in the town. We can be fairly sure Mary did not do this. Certainly, it would have been out of the question for her to spend her nights at the Van Lew house; to have gone back and forth from there would have attracted suspicion to both herself and to Elizabeth, who was, as both women knew, already being closely watched. So it is quite likely Mary was one of those who shared the makeshift accommodation in the sheds.

Davis often worked at home late into the night, when everyone else was in bed, and only went to bed himself in the small hours. Was his office ever left unlocked at such times? Did Mary sometimes find her way into that inner room, while the secretary who by day guarded access to the president slept on the floor above? Or did she go into the office in the daytime to clean while the president and his secretary were away, and seize the chance to look around?

The Confederate president, famous for bringing his work home to the domestic office, was notorious for leaving official papers strewn about on chairs and tables in the family quarters, for the servants to tidy away. Who apart from himself and Burton Harrison, his utterly loyal secretary, would be likely to read those documents? His wife might catch a glimpse, but that would not greatly matter. Catherine the nanny would hardly be interested, and in any case spent all her time with the children in the nursery. Varina's personal maid was illiterate. And so, it was assumed, was the young woman Mary—the girl, Varina would have called her—who came up and down the stairs from time to time, bearing trays and polishing the furniture.

The part Mary was playing required her to appear blind to the written word, and in this house, it was everywhere—on the covers of books and magazines, in the daily newspapers, on mail envelopes, on government documents and military dispatches, and on the labels of tins and packets on kitchen shelves. It took only one slip to suggest she could recognize these supposedly incomprehensible strings of letters, and suspicions would ripple through the household, threatening her safety.

Mary's life in the Davis household could not have been easy. She was assumed to be a slave, and even if fairly well treated, she was still marked with that lowly status. Mary had always been bold and talkative. She had been a free child at school in the North, learning among her peers, and then, in Liberia, a free teenager, trusted to educate others. She was a married woman and well into her twenties now, but she was ordered about and referred to as a "girl."

All the household servants were expected to be up and about in the small hours, cleaning out grates, lighting fires, making hot drinks for family and guests still in bed, heating water, laying the table for breakfast, taking down washing left drying overnight in the scullery, and carrying in goods from carts coming into the yard and putting everything away. Then there were outer steps to sweep and scrub before visitors arrived.

As usual in wealthy homes, the Davis household had a definite social hierarchy. The kitchen maids helped the cook with chopping and mincing, scrubbing work tables, and scouring pans. There were other basement drudges, who did the plentiful heavy labor below stairs. Above these maids-of-all-work at the bottom of the pyramid came those like Mary—the "upstairs" servants, who waited at table and took round trays at receptions, fetched and carried to upper floors, helped clear away after dinners and parties, dusted, swept, polished, and tidied away things carelessly strewn about, and generally made themselves useful, as unobtrusively as possible.

Above Mary's social level came those servants with definite skills like the cook, the coachman, and Jefferson's personal valet and Varina's maid. Although these attendants were lowly slaves, and regarded as such by their masters, they were valued and trusted, and would have considered themselves a cut above the other slaves, and even some of the paid servants. At the apex of the domestic pyramid came the white Europeans—Catherine the Irish nanny, Mary O'Melia the housekeeper, the steward Eggeling, and Burton Harrison the secretary, who, although a salaried employee, was regarded by the Davises as a friend and practically a member of the family.

Even with some servants boarding out and others spending their nights in the sheds in the garden, it was a crowded house. In the daytime, at least when there were no important visitors, the Davises' young children had the run of the place. The eldest boy liked to play out in the garden, wearing his little Confederate uniform, setting up targets and firing at "Yankees" with a real miniature cannon someone had given him. At the same time, soldiers and politicians were constantly coming into the house on official business, bearing messages or seeking private interviews. Private citizens also came in hope of a favor from the president—a commission in the army, a promotion, or a reprieve for a family member accused of taking bribes.

Friends and relatives came to call on Varina, and sometimes stayed a night or more. When the Davises had lived in the house a year, Varina's recently widowed mother arrived to join the household, and then Varina's younger sister Margaret came to stay. She was quick-witted and quarrelsome, and not afraid to make public scenes. Her presence proved a constant source of embarrassment to both Varina and her husband.

Varina's friends visited often, and sat chatting with her in the snug, while coffee and hot chocolate were brought to them. One of the closest of these friends was Mary Chesnut, mentioned above. Mary was an astute, observant woman, who shared with Varina an enjoyment of reading and of discussing what she read. Another good friend was Judah Benjamin, a member of Davis's cabinet, who at different times served the Confederacy as attorney general, secretary of war, and secretary of state. He would often come to the house on business, but stay afterwards to talk with Varina. The two were, perhaps, drawn together by their mutual sense of being outsiders—she half a Northerner, and he a Jew. They exchanged society gossip, no doubt, but part of that gossip would have been to do with political intrigues, or the misdeeds and failings of Confederate generals and the conduct of the war. A servant, moving quietly in and out of the snug with cups and teapots, would potentially hear things the friends would not want repeated outside of that room.

Although the Davises did not host large, public, open-house gatherings, there was still plenty of activity in their household. Mary would have been in constant demand amid the comings and goings of soldiers and civilians for meetings and private conferences, the occasional select dinners and parties, the noisy romping of the children, the calls for service from Varina and her friends in their cozy inner room. She went about her days bringing in clean dishes and clearing away dirty ones, bending to pick up children's toys, dusting and rearranging ornaments on the shelves; but except when someone demanded service from her, she was wholly ignored and disregarded—an unnoticed feature of the domestic background.

In this busy, exhausting world, Mary lived, served, and spied all through the long years of the Civil War. It must at times have felt as if it would never end. Aching back and swollen ankles were the least of it. In that lonely position, living by her wits, there was no one in the household she could confide in. And she could never relax her guard. If she were caught listening in too carefully to a conversation, or paying more attention to the words on a page than might be expected of an illiterate person, or caught in a room where she was not supposed to be, the game would be up. Even at night, she was not safe: What if she talked in her sleep, and someone overheard her? And if she were caught, she could expect no mercy from Jefferson Davis. When one of his trusted slaves ran away and was reported to have given intelligence to the Union military, a warrant was immediately issued for his arrest. If Mary had been caught spying in Davis's own household, it is unlikely that even the Van Lew women with their elite social connections could have done anything to save her.

How did she keep her nerve through all those months? Her years before the war as a child far from home in an unfamiliar town, and as a teenage missionary, living among strangers in an alien land, had bred in her a habit of relying on her own resources that stood her in good stead now. She might also have gained courage from knowing of others who were risking their lives in the cause of freedom—not only Elizabeth Van Lew's agents around Richmond, but fellow spies she would never meet, in towns and military encampments across the South. Many of these dedicated workers for the Union cause were black.

Blacks, particularly the enslaved, had one great advantage in working undercover—they were consistently underestimated by the whites who controlled their lives. Mary Louvestre, housekeeper to a military engineer at the Gosport Navy Yard in Norfolk, Virginia, was a case in point. She managed to run away from her white master and make it up to the Union lines where she reported on the Confederates' plan to build an ironclad steam ship. Another former slave (her name is lost to history, but her husband's name was Dabney) volunteered as a camp washerwoman to a Confederate general to spy on the troops under his command. Robert Smalls was a slave who worked as a pilot in the harbor at Charleston, South Carolina. He later escaped, and reported to the federal government on the state of naval forces in the port. Harriet Tubman, famous for her extraordinary heroism in guiding hundreds of slaves to freedom by repeated ventures into slave-holding territory, also served the Union cause in military terms. On one occasion, in June 1863, she led a contingent of black U.S. soldiers on a raid on Combahee Ferry to seize an ammunition store, resulting in the liberation of 750 enslaved people. Tubman, like Mary Richards Bowser, also regularly supplied Union commanders with valuable intelligence.

The councils of war that took place in the state dining room of the White House of the Confederacy often went on well into the small hours. One such meeting, in the spring of 1862, was convened to address a crisis in the conduct of the war. Union troops were besieging the key strategic port of Yorktown, 60 miles from Richmond, where Confederate forces were heavily outnumbered. A series of clever ruses by the Confederate commander John Magruder had held them off for several weeks, but it was clear the standoff could not last. On April 14, the situation was serious enough for key military leaders—Joseph Johnston, Robert E. Lee, James Longstreet, and Gustavus Smith—to assemble round the table in Davis's upstairs dining room. The secretary of war, George Wythe Randolph was also there. Apart from Jefferson Davis, he was the only civilian present.

The meeting began at 7 p.m. and dragged on until well after midnight as the generals argued over how to deal with the threat. If Yorktown fell, they knew that Richmond would be next. The debate grew heated; voices were raised as the contending generals struggled to win the argument, oblivious of everything else. They would hardly have noticed the servant among them, slipping quietly in and out of the room, bringing coffee and clearing away spent cigars. One can well imagine Mary hovering by the sideboard, taking her time to refill a water jug, or reaching down to take something from a cupboard. She was always there, somewhere in the background, unnoticed, but noting everything. (In the event, thanks predominantly to the Union generals' mistakes and hesitations, the Confederate forces evaded the besiegers at Yorktown and beat a tactical retreat.)

Within the questioning, intellectual environment of Princeton's black community, Mary had been encouraged to form strong opinions and have the courage to voice them. But her constantly changing life had made her adaptable too, with the ability to adjust to new and challenging circumstances. It had made her discreet and careful in how she related to others. She had to get along with the other servants. She had to please Mary O'Melia, and to think twice, and then a third time, before opening her mouth to speak. She had to anticipate people's moods. As she would remark later in a different context, "scrutinizing" the expressions on people's faces became an ingrained habit.

Down in the kitchen, the servants gossiped, sharing rumors and shreds of information. "They say General Lee's going to Yorktown." "You don't know that." "What did Mr. Davis say?" "What if the Yankees take Yorktown? Are the Yankees coming here?" Though Mary might have answered many of these questions, she would have had to hold her tongue. Where lives were at stake, she knew how to keep her head lowered, and her eyes and ears alert. She would also have to hide her anxiety about what might happen should the Confederacy win the war. At the start, it seemed that this would, indeed, be the outcome. Then there would be no end to slavery, ever.

For the war's first two years, Mary followed events "with almost a broken heart," as she later said.[11] Yet, however she suffered in her feelings about the war, and the stifling, stressful role she was compelled to play, she had a task to perform, and would not abandon it. Because of her courage and commitment, a steady flow of compromising intelligence seeped out of the Davis mansion and found its way to the Union lines.

By 1864, a year before the war's end, Elizabeth Van Lew had come fully to know the worth of Mary Richards Bowser. She kept alert for the stream of vital intelligence from that source. "How lives the outside world!" Elizabeth confided to her journal, "When I open my eyes in the morning, I say to the servant, 'What news, Mary?' and my caterer never fails!"[12]

In September 1864, another top-secret meeting of Confederate generals took place at the White House of the Confederacy, this time concerning the vulnerability of their forces around Richmond. The argument in favor of a tactical retreat won a degree of support around the table, and this crucial piece of intelligence, indicative of the weakness of the Confederates' position, was relayed to General Ulysses S. Grant, commander of the Union forces. Feeling emboldened, he decided to launch an all-out attack.

As the tide of war turned against the South, their commanders found themselves out-maneuvered at every turn. The Union generals seemed almost telepathically to anticipate their movements, so much so that the Confederate leadership began to suspect that someone was leaking information, and that the leaks were coming from inside their own White House. With the benefit of hindsight, it appears odd that Davis was so slow to wonder whether the culprit might be Mary Richards Bowser. But why should anyone suspect an illiterate housemaid? Mary carried on drudging for the Davises undetected, seen by everyone, and yet disregarded—hidden in plain sight.

Thomas McNiven

Mary was the best ...

—Union secret agent Thomas McNiven[1]

Mary may have felt isolated in her undercover role in the Davis household, but she was not completely cut off from the outside world. Her link to the Van Lew house on Church Hill—one might almost say her lifeline—was the friendly face of a local pastry cook, Christopher Taylor. Taylor, a freed black man, did the baking for Thomas McNiven, a naturalized U.S. citizen who had come from Glasgow with his two brothers eight years before the war, and opened a liquor store in Brooklyn.

As a Scot with republican sympathies, McNiven had an implacable hatred of slavery. He quickly became active in the U.S. abolitionist movement, which led to his first visit to Richmond in July 1855, to make contact with anti-slavery activists in the Scottish community there. McNiven then began working with the underground railroad, ferrying fugitive slaves out of Virginia. He hid them, three abreast, in the bottom of his false-bottomed wagon.

When the Civil War began, McNiven moved to settle in Richmond, where he quickly built up a wide network of contacts, beginning with the Scottish and German communities, of which many members were opposed to slavery and the Confederacy. With the help of funding from Northern abolitionists and the embryonic U.S. Secret Service, he opened a bakery, specializing in biscuits and shortbread, at 811, North 5th Street, roughly a mile from Mary Richards Bowser's place of work. It was the perfect front for a spying operation. McNiven and his employee Christopher Taylor were soon busy gathering intelligence for the Union on their deliveries all around the city, including, with Mary's help, at the White House of the Confederacy.

Thomas McNiven claimed that by the end of the war, he was in touch with over 300 Unionist sympathizers in and around Richmond. One of the most important was surely Elizabeth Van Lew. In 1862, as worshipers were coming out after a service at St. John's Church (a popular meeting place for Union sympathizers), one of Elizabeth's contacts, a man named Haskins, pointed McNiven out to her as "a friend to be trusted." It was to be the start of a fruitful collaboration.

While he operated his own independent spy ring, McNiven recognized the merit of joining forces on occasion with Van Lew, given her efficiency, her social connections, and her ability to infiltrate key departments in the Confederate government. He would approach her in the churchyard outside St. John's after a Sunday service, and discreetly they would exchange information and talk about developments in the war. For those who did not want to be seen speaking with suspected Unionists, messages could be hidden in crevices in broken gravestones, to be retrieved later. A motley gathering of abolitionists, Union loyalists, and active Union agents would turn up there, including Presbyterians, Lutherans, and Quakers. They had a visual code by which to identify one another, using badges carved from peach stones in the shape of clover leaves. The clover leaf could be turned around on the badge. "When it was upside down," McNiven said, "it was safe to talk. When it was right side up, not safe." (The MS collection at the Library of Virginia contains both the McNiven memoir and a photograph of one of the clover leaf badges.)

Van Lew became one of McNiven's most valuable allies. "She had contacts everywhere," he said. He recalled particularly that she "got us the plans for all the rebel lines east of Richmond in 1864," adding that "[Major General Benjamin] Butler could have marched right into the city, but he dragged and dragged and the opportunity was lost." McNiven also remembered how Van Lew organized the prison escape of two Union officers, Colonels Thomas Rose and Abel Streight, "almost alone." But in spite of mutual admiration, the relationship between McNiven and Van Lew was never, it seems, one of total trust on either side. McNiven recalls that Elizabeth, ever cautious and protective of others' safety, always refused to tell him the identities of her agents. He, in turn, spied on the spy. He and his agents broke the code she had designed for her messages so that he could read what she sent before passing it on. "We never let her know," he said. All the same, McNiven spoke of his affection for Elizabeth Van Lew, which endured long after the war. After her death in 1900, he said, "I stayed at her grave for hours, long after all her family left. It was like I lost my mother."

Such was McNiven's confidence in Elizabeth Van Lew that he took considerable risks to assist her in her activities. Once he almost got caught going north with plans she had supplied of Confederate troop movements. As he recalled, thankfully, "My British papers and my tobacco buying orders from Lorillard got me safely up and back." He also described some of the methods employed by his agents in the "Richmond ring." He tells, for instance, of bribes used to organize riots in the town—"a lot of dollars American" went into orchestrating these—and of getting Richmond munitions workers at the city arsenal to "fix up some very bad ammunition from time to time." His agents paid railroad employees to misdirect strategically vital war materiel. "Most all of the rebels would take bribes," he said, "if it was in good USA, not their, money, or gold." He also supplied Van Lew with funds to help persuade those who were reluctant to cooperate.

McNiven's is an oral testimony first told to his daughter Jeanette and finally written down by his grandson, Robert Waitt, after his death in 1904. Its accuracy, therefore, has sometimes been called into question. Facts have no doubt been omitted, exaggerated, or otherwise altered in the telling, but on the other hand, its sheer wealth of detail—including lists of agents with their codenames, dates of events that can be checked with the historical record, and details of the lives and acquaintances of members of his Richmond network—suggests a largely faithful account.

What lends particular credibility to the McNiven memoir is the circumstantial information that links him to Elizabeth Van Lew. He knew, for example, about Elizabeth's friendship with the Swedish novelist Fredrika Bremer—"the Swede writer," as he called her. He knew the name of Bremer's sister in Philadelphia, who passed on the novelist's letters to Elizabeth. When Van Lew wanted to write back, he said, "we would smuggle out her reply letters." It seems unlikely that he would be aware of Bremer's contact with Elizabeth, let alone the identity of one of Bremer's relatives, unless he had known Elizabeth quite well. He also told of her connection with Mr. Haskins, the same man who had pointed him out to her as a possible trustworthy ally. Haskins had owned the Libby warehouse before it became a prison, and "knew every inch of it," said McNiven. Haskins, he said, was "a big help to Miss Van Lew when she went there." McNiven even tells of the origin of the double-bottomed custard dish that Elizabeth used to carry messages in and out of the prison, saying it belonged to a German woman named Johannah Hoffmann. "She had brought it with her from Bavaria when she and Philipe Hoffmann came to America." (Incidentally, after the war, McNiven would marry Johannah's daughter Emelia.)

The method McNiven describes for contacting Mary Richards Bowser in the White House of the Confederacy is entirely credible. When making deliveries there, Christopher Taylor, McNiven's assistant, would wait outside with his wagon for Mary to come out and tell him what she had learned since his last visit. If Mary found it unsafe to go to the Church Hill mansion herself, Taylor or McNiven would presumably relay the information to Elizabeth Van Lew.

Towards the end of the war, Thomas McNiven had begun to feel vulnerable:

> The rebels got very suspicious of me in January of 1865. They picked me up three times and were very rough in questioning me, but couldn't get me to say anything and let me go. I figured it was time to get out of Richmond and [I] left everything in Miss Van Lew's hands.

He seems to have had particular admiration for the women who helped him in his intelligence work. They were a diverse group. In addition to Elizabeth Van Lew and the women of the German community, he kept in contact with a woman named Clara, the favorite prostitute of a member of the Confederate cabinet. Clara revealed that her client was stealing municipal money to fund his visits to prostitutes, stirring up conflict between the Confederate administration and the Richmond city council. "She should have a monument," McNiven said. And then there was Mary.

"Mary was the best," said McNiven; "she was working right in Davis' house." The significance of some of the intelligence she managed to collect was extraordinary, even to him. He recalled, "One time, when Chris took some tea biscuits to Davis' house, little Mary had the terms that the rebels were offering at Hampton Roads to Lincoln's men to end the war."

The abortive Hampton Roads negotiations between Lincoln and the Confederate leaders took place in February 1865, only eight weeks before the South surrendered, suggesting that Mary Richards Bowser must have stayed at her post until very nearly the bitter end. (This is, however, contradicted by Mary's own claim that she left Richmond in the fall of 1864—which could have been as late as November that year, just weeks before the Hampton Roads meeting. It is possible that these Confederate peace terms—to which McNiven retrospectively applied the name "Hampton Roads"—were secretly circulating months before the actual meeting, and Mary had got to know of them.) Whatever the actual timing of the leak, we know that Elizabeth Van Lew arranged for the details of these rebel peace terms to be circulated all over Richmond, causing severe embarrassment to the Southern leadership. The Confederates were "sick about it," said McNiven.

If McNiven is more than a trifle patronizing in his description of Mary— "little Mary," he called her, even though at twenty-six when the war began he was not much older than she was—he also expressed his respect for her abilities as a spy. She had, he said admiringly, a "photographic" mind: "Everything she saw on the Rebel President's desk she could repeat word for word."

Mary may or may not have had a photographic memory. She could simply have been good at reading over a document to get the gist of it, and summarizing what she read. A training in reading comprehension and précis was, after all, an essential part of any nineteenth-century education; and her time at school in Princeton would have given her intensive practice in those skills. What McNiven knew, was that she not only kept her eyes and ears open, but could assimilate and accurately recall large chunks of written information. As McNiven freely admitted, some of the most useful information ever gathered by the Richmond intelligence network, was supplied by "little Mary" Richards.

6

Things Fall Apart

Bless the Lord, the Yankees have come!

—Seventeen-year-old Amy Spain, who paid
for these joyful words with her life

By 1863, it was clear to anyone who cared to think about it, that the war was not going well for the Confederacy. With hindsight—but even at the time for those who followed closely the fortunes of the contending armies—the Union capture of Vicksburg on the Mississippi River was a turning point in Confederate fortunes, giving the Union forces effective control of the Deep South.

In Richmond, 1863 and 1864 were grim for everyone, even the wealthy. The draining of the treasury by the costs of the war, combined with the Union's naval blockade of Southern ports, led to soaring prices and widespread shortages. Additionally, it did not help the Confederate cause that Jefferson Davis was often in conflict with his generals, criticizing them constantly for their conduct of the war. Davis, who would have preferred to be directing operations from the back of a horse rather than running the government, annoyed the field commanders by his constant attempts to micromanage military operations. To the dismay of his aides, on at least one occasion he put himself at risk by going to the field of battle to observe the fighting in person.

Davis was at loggerheads with one commander in particular, Joseph "Joe" Johnston. Popular with the private soldiers and with his own officers, the general was resented by Davis for his assertive attitudes. "The President detests Joe Johnston for all the trouble he has given him," Mary Chesnut noted in her diary; "and General Joe returns the compliment with compound interest. His hatred of Jeff Davis amounts to a religion. With him it colors all things."

In the military encampments, as on the home front, provisions began to be in short supply. According to Varina Davis, even the soldiers at the battlefront were at risk of malnutrition. In January 1863, Robert E. Lee wrote to the secretary of war that his army was not sufficiently well fed to fight in the spring campaign. Lee recommended the suspension of the officers' privileges that allowed them to buy food supplies at a discount. The president's own family had no such special entitlement, Varina claimed, but bought their provisions in the town like any other citizens, and at the current prices.

The government decreed fast days as an appeal to religious devotion, presumably, but also to save on food. The upper classes hosted "starvation parties" and dinners, where dancing and music were provided, but the only refreshments on offer were bread and water. All the same, a year before the war ended, the Davis family was still eating well. In February 1864, Varina was able to give a lunch for her female friends with a menu of "Gumbo, ducks and olives, chickens in jelly, oysters, lettuce salad, chocolate cream, jelly and cake," washed down with claret and champagne.[1]

Other Richmond citizens resorted to all kinds of devices to cope with shortages of food and clothing. Housewives concocted a coffee substitute from parched sweet potatoes and parched corn. Sorghum syrup became a substitute for sugar. People used old carpet material to fashion makeshift shoes with canvas soles. They donated their carpets, too, to provide blankets for the army, making do with cotton blankets for themselves.

Varina praised the ingenuity that went into improvising attractive clothing:

The ladies made themselves natty little gloves embroidered beautifully.... They covered their worn-out shoes with pieces of silk and satin, drawn from old boxes long unused; old scraps of silk were cut in strips, picked to pieces, carded and spun into fine yarn, and silk stockings knitted from it. The most beautiful hats were plaited from palmetto, dried and bleached, as well as from straw. The feathers from domestic fowls were so treated that they were very decorative to their bonnets....

Even affluent families were struggling. Finding himself short of money, Jefferson Davis sold three of his horses. He also sold two people. The unfortunate slaves fetched just $1,612 in Confederate money.[2] Davis also hired out slaves from his Brierfield estate in Mississippi to work on the military fortifications at Vicksburg. Four of these men died working on the defenses.

In late April 1862, New Orleans fell to the Union forces. Varina's family members in the area fled to Georgia. Then the Union army moved into Mississippi, and captured Brierfield. Several slaves left the plantation at this point, including the family of Ben Montgomery. Ben had been an overseer, and one of the enslaved workers Davis liked and trusted the most.

In the Davises' Richmond mansion, meanwhile, there was another defection. The enslaved coachman, William Jackson, who had been hired out to the Davises by a Richmond resident for $250 a year, had decamped to Union-held territory on April 27, 1862, leaving behind his wife and three children. At the time, Jackson's flight probably seemed to Davis no more than an annoyance, but it would prove to have damaging consequences for Davis's reputation in the long run.

By late May, Richmond residents had other things to worry about than runaway slaves. There was alarm in the Davis household, and across the whole city, as news spread that Union commander George McLellan was closing in on Richmond. Union warships were advancing up the James River. "The panic began some days later," Varina recalled. "It was pitiable to see our friends coming in without anything except the clothes they had on, and mourning the loss of their trunks in a piteous jumble of pain and worriment."

Everywhere, the talk was of evacuation. Richmond residents were burying their valuables and bundling up their belongings with a view to fleeing the town. Jefferson Davis told his wife to leave too. "Always averse to flight, I entreated him to grant a little delay," Varina recalled; "but he was firm." Reluctantly, she obeyed: "I communicated the news to the family." Varina left with her children on May 10 for Raleigh, North Carolina, still in Confederate hands. They stayed with other fugitives there, in a school for girls.

After a brief battle, the enemy warships withdrew. "Richmond breathed freer," Varina said. However, for seven days after the naval encounter, there was still fierce fighting uncomfortably close to the town. The stench of cannon smoke drifted over the streets.

By the first week in July, however, the crisis was over. The Union forces withdrew, and Varina came home.

While the fighting raged in Virginia, William Jackson, the fugitive coachman, had been busy in New York, giving interviews to the pro-abolition newspapers *Harper's Weekly* and *The New York Tribune*. He told what little he knew about the state of Richmond's defenses, and perhaps more significantly, about the low morale of Richmond's citizens. Jackson also described Jefferson Davis's state of mind. The Confederate president, he said, was "pale and haggard," suffering from insomnia— "eating nothing, constantly irritable"—and full of complaints about his generals. "He plans advances, but they execute masterly retreats," Jackson was quoted as saying.[3]

A little later, news of another scandal within the Davis household began to spread. A slave named Dick, hired out to the Davises, was arrested as part of a banknote forgery ring. Slaves, it seemed—if not on the run or quietly engaging in spying—were becoming unreliable, even in the Confederate president's own household.

Then, in January 1863, came the Emancipation Proclamation:

> That on the first day of January in the year of our Lord, one thousand eight hundred and sixty-three, all persons held as slaves within any State, or designated part of a State, the people whereof shall then be in rebellion against the United States shall be then, thenceforward, and forever free; and the executive government of the United States, including the military and naval authority thereof, will recognize and maintain the freedom of such persons, and will do no act or acts to repress such persons, or any of them, in any efforts they may make for their actual freedom.

The bid to free slaves, which had begun as purely an opportunistic move on the part of the federal government, now blazed up as a beacon of hope to the millions held in bondage. True, the proclamation declared only some slaves free—in those states in active insurrection against the Union. It was hoped that the enslaved in these areas would rise up, run away, and join the fight against their oppressors.

Even eighteen months later, as the war dragged on and Lincoln was campaigning for re-election, some Northern African Americans expressed disillusionment with the president's decidedly patchy record on opposing slavery, preferring to express their support for the "Radical Democrat" candidate John Fremont. Lincoln, wrote one contributor to the New York-based paper, the *Weekly Anglo-African*, was "fickle-minded" and compromising. He claimed that while "holding anti-slavery principles in one hand and colonization in the other, [the president] always gave concessions to slavery when the Union could be preserved without touching the peculiar institution."[4] However, not surprisingly—even though the promise of freedom applied only to some enslaved people and not others—the Emancipation Proclamation aroused alarm and fury among whites all across the South, and hopeful anticipation among blacks everywhere.

In the black Southern communities, the word spread. Those few who could read told the news to those who could not. In areas still under Confederate control, enslaved people passed the news on in whispers. Mary Richards Bowser, at her post in the White House of the Confederacy and tuned in to a city-wide intelligence network, was privy to the indignant conversations of Mr. and Mrs. Jefferson Davis and their friends, and the displeasure of white citizens from across Richmond. If ever her eye fell upon a front page of a Virginia newspaper denouncing this latest outrage of the federal government, she surely shared in the thrill of hope that ran through all African-American hearts.

Varina, of course, thought differently. "Philanthropists and agitators" might be pleased by the proclamation, she said, but she could only view it as politically motivated. "At a single dash of the pen," she wrote, the proclamation attempted to "annihilate four hundred billions of our property," to "disrupt the whole social structure of the South," and "to pour over the country a flood of evils many times greater than the loss of property."

There would be more departures of slaves from Varina's home in Richmond (accelerated, no doubt, by the hopes inspired by the Emancipation Proclamation). Early in 1863, a year after the William Jackson incident, Varina's personal maidservant Betsey ran away in company with her husband Jim Pemberton, son of a Brierfield overseer. Before leaving, Betsey had simply told Varina that she was "going out for a while," letting it be assumed that she had some errand to run and would be back shortly. "We never saw her afterward," Varina said. The fact that Betsey and her husband were not "hired servants," owned by someone else and sent to work with the Davises, but born into slavery within the Davis household and regarded by them almost as family members, would have made their defection all the more disturbing. Betsey in particular was, in Varina's words, "an object of much affectionate solicitude to me." At her disappearance, she was "filled with grave apprehensions" for "the poor creature's safety." (Did Betsey and Jim, one wonders, ever think in such fond terms about their former mistress?)

Mary Chesnut was less surprised than Varina at the departure of these favored servants. "It is miraculous," she observed, "that they had the fortitude to resist temptation so long ... I do not think it had ever crossed Mrs. Davis's brain that these two could leave her." In common with many other white Southerners, Chesnut was convinced the couple's flight could only be motivated by greed. They must have been bribed by Unionists, she thought, who hoped to get information from them. Someone had told her that Betsey had left with $80 in gold in her possession, and $2,400 in Confederate notes. "First they were seen with gold galore," Chesnut wrote in her diary, "and then they would fly to the Yankees, and I am sure they had nothing to tell. It is Yankee money wasted."

Two weeks after the departure of Betsey and Jim, a fire broke out in the basement of the White House of the Confederacy. The Davises happened to be entertaining guests at the time, so Varina's reception party turned out to be "a sensational one," as Mary Chesnut noted ironically. The fire seemed to have been set deliberately. It was quickly put out, but there was no trace of the arsonist, or arsonists. The excited guests traded theories about their identity. They were, it was said, either "the usual bribed servants," or "some escaped Yankee prisoners," but their true identity was anyone's guess. A practical-minded journalist, reporting the incident in the *Richmond Examiner*, wondered why the culprit(s) had not waited till the guests had gone home and the household were all in bed. Perhaps, Chesnut reflected dryly, "the arson contingent"—she seems to have imagined a collective conspiracy behind the blaze—"will wait and do better next time":

> Fancy having to be always ready to have your servants set your house on fire, being bribed to do it. Such constant robberies, such servants coming and going daily to the Yankees, carrying one's silver, one's other possessions, does not conduce to home happiness.[5]

Popular legend has attributed responsibility for the arson attempt (if that is what it was) to Mary Richards Bowser. But why would a woman operating undercover want to draw any such blatant attention to herself?

Shortly after the fire incident, Henry, the Davises' butler, quietly slipped away. In February, a man named Cornelius, another slave hired out to the Davis mansion, had also decamped, allegedly helping himself to supplies from the pantry on his way out. A story about Cornelius in *The Daily South Carolinian* claimed that the fugitive "had his pockets stuffed with money, preserves, ham, chicken, and biscuit, showing how kindly he was treated, or else how great a rogue he was." "These continual elopements," the article went on, "induce the belief that Mr. Davis'[s] negroes are tampered with by abolitionists."[6]

Everywhere in the rebel states, the Emancipation Proclamation was making its effects felt. As Varina said, and with uncharacteristic understatement, "the condition" of their slaves in Mississippi began to be "unsettled." The most obvious manifestation of this "unsettled" mood became apparent when, in the summer of that year, Brierfield plantation once again fell into Union hands, and a Union army officer assured the Brierfield slaves that they were now free. This time, it was more than a handful of them who voted with their feet. Almost the whole workforce of 137 went, leaving behind only six adults and a few children. The fugitives headed for newly captured Vicksburg, many taking Davis's property with them, carted off from the estate. (Back wages, one might say, for all the years of unpaid forced labor.)

Varina's first reaction to these accumulating defections was incredulity. How could servants, as she preferred to call them, be so ungrateful as to rob their "kindly" masters and run away? She again took refuge in the popular myth that the root cause of the slave exodus was bribery. The fugitives—now free men and women—if they had not actually been abducted against their will, must have been seduced by people paid to encourage them. She firmly believed the stories about "clubs of disaffected colored men in Richmond, generally presided over by a white man," who could earn $2,000 "for each servant who ran off from our service." For incredulous slave owners, only financial inducements could ever persuade their supposedly loyal underlings to walk away.

With Union troops now only miles from Richmond and getting nearer by the day, enslaved people hardly needed abolitionists to tell them what to do. Freedom was within their grasp and many chose to take it. Some would join up to fight for the Union. Of the estimated half a million who fled from bondage during the Civil War, thousands had already joined the federal armies.

One thing was certain—the repeated defections gave the lie, once and for all, to the myth of the contented slave. No doubt those enslaved people who were fed well and treated relatively humanely had been resigned to staying put in captivity when they saw no alternative, reflecting that their situation under a different master could be so much worse. (And if they did have thoughts of running away, the penalties for getting caught were terrifying.) Escape from bondage now looked ever more possible, however. The U.S. president himself had proclaimed the slaves free, at least in those states actively at war with the Union. Then what was there to keep them? The prospect of freedom—in spite of danger and hardship—had to look preferable to slavery, even under the most benign masters.

Varina, however, still could not understand it. In the early years of the war, she had often expressed both pity and contempt for those who ran away. In an October 1862 edition of a Washington newspaper, she read of the plight of escaped slaves, living crowded together in makeshift accommodation in towns under Union control. There were thousands of them in the Virginia town of Alexandria alone, the article reported—unemployed, homeless, hungry, and at risk of infectious diseases. The implied moral the reader was intended to draw, was that the unfortunates would have been better off remaining in slavery.[7] The article described the plight of escaped slaves who, in October 1862, could not claim the status of free men and women. They were known as "contrabands"—still regarded as property and kept as such by the Union forces until the end of the war when the question of the slaveholding system could be resolved. If the South had won the war, these contrabands would have been returned to slavery. The favored Betsey, who had left the Davises a year after the Emancipation Proclamation with her husband, would not have become a "contraband" but a free individual. It must have seemed a prize worth the taking.[8]

In spite of all evidence to the contrary—the mass slave exodus from his own plantation, for instance—Jefferson Davis continued to think that talk about "the horrors of slavery" was all nonsense. While their white owners were away at the war, had not the slaves carried on working as usual?

> Had these Africans been a cruelly oppressed people, restlessly struggling to be freed from their bonds, would their masters have dared to leave them, as was done, and would they have remained as they did, continuing their usual duties, or could the proclamation of emancipation have been put on the plea of a military necessity, if the fact had been that the negroes were forced to serve, and desired only an opportunity to rise against their masters? [9]

Meanwhile, the tide of war continued to turn against the Confederacy, and General Joseph Johnston continued to be at odds with Jefferson Davis. The mutual suspicion between them was intense. "Joe Johnston does not exactly say that Jeff Davis betrays his plans to the enemy, but he says he dares not let the President know his plans, as there is a spy in the War Office who invariably warns the Yankees in time." If, in this observation, Mary Chesnut was implying that Johnston was simply paranoid or making excuses for his military failures, the general almost certainly knew better. There may well have been an agent in the War Office. The Richmond spy ring, as we have seen, was highly efficient, and Union agents were strategically posted everywhere; even under the president's own roof. For Mary Richards Bowser, being a Union spy was now more dangerous than ever. "In the red hot state our public mind now is in," Mary Chesnut noted in her diary, "there will be a short shrift for spies." In February 1864, the *Richmond Examiner* reported on the hanging of a captured Union spy, Spencer Deaton, at Castle Thunder.[10] The witch hunt had begun.

An abortive attempt, at the end of February 1864, to organize a mass breakout of captured Union soldiers held in Libby Prison led to a wave of public paranoia. Elizabeth Van Lew was deeply implicated in this doomed operation, dubbed "the Dahlgren raid." The Union officer Ulric Dahlgren rode in from Union-held territory in a bid to free the prisoners. Dahlgren was ambushed and killed, and the rescue party never even managed to enter Richmond. Papers allegedly found on his body were said to convict him of a plan to assassinate Jefferson Davis. While Unionist sympathizers insisted (possibly correctly) that the documents were forged, there were plenty in Richmond more than willing to believe them genuine. Southern newspapers seized on the sensational story, working their readers into a lather of indignation over the alleged murder threat against their president. Elizabeth Van Lew noted the effect on public opinion:

> The forged papers said to have been found on Colonel Dahlgren's body had maddened the people, and Southern people when maddened, who have been used to giving way to wrath with violence on negroes, stop not at trifles. A slave population (defenseless) tempts a people, should right offend them, to be passionate and regardless of consequences.

Van Lew was in no doubt that in the wake of the supposed assassination attempt, whether genuine or not, repression was bound to follow.

In April 1864, Elizabeth received an anonymous threatening message from the "White Caps," a forerunner of the Ku Klux Klan: "Old maid. Is your house insured? Put this in the fire and mum's the word." In late September, the Van Lews, mother and daughter, found themselves under intensified scrutiny as police pressured acquaintances to testify against Elizabeth. Later in the year, on September 27, 1864, Elizabeth's sister-in-law was questioned. John Van Lew's wife reported that Elizabeth was "a strong abolitionist," and that she hoped for a Union victory. Moreover, Elizabeth and her mother had, she reported, "sent a negro woman North to be educated."

Nothing more could be convincingly alleged against Elizabeth, however, and her status as a Southern lady from a highly respected family protected her, as did her sex. It was assumed that she, like most women, was apt to speak thoughtlessly and to change her mind on a whim. When the Van Lew case landed on his desk at the adjutant general's office, Judge Advocate Charles Blackford shared this prevailing view. While acknowledging Elizabeth's "unfriendly sentiments" towards the Confederacy, he stated that in his opinion she had not actually "done anything" to damage the Southern cause. With typical feminine indiscretion, she had, "like most of her sex," spoken too freely, and spitefully her in-laws had taken advantage of her foolish talk to inform on her. "No action to be taken," Blackford wrote.

All the same, in the house on Church Hill, a climate of fear now prevailed:

> With shutters closed and curtains pinned together, how have we been startled at the barking of a dog and drawn nearer together, the pallor coming over our faces and the blood rushing to our hearts.... Then to follow the innocent visitor to the door, to lower the gas as, with muffled face, they said good night and the last words often were, "Do you think I am watched?"[11]

If people like Elizabeth enjoyed a good deal of protection owing to their social status, others were not so fortunate. In January 1865, as the Union commander William Sherman headed steadily north towards Virginia following his recent capture of Savannah, Georgia, and the Union armies prepared to close in on Richmond, there was a wholesale rounding up of pro-Union agents. Ten men who had played leading roles in escape networks and intelligence gathering were arrested and imprisoned.

Blacks everywhere in the South, and at all times, were particularly vulnerable. In Darlington, South Carolina, on March 10, 1865, Amy Spain, a seventeen-year-old slave, was arrested after she had taken abandoned Confederate property in the town and led others to join her in carrying it away. When Union troops retreated and Confederate forces returned, she was tried and hanged in public from a tree outside the courthouse. She was executed less for the theft than, in the words of the charge sheet, for "treason and conduct unbecoming a slave." Her "treason" apparently consisted of exclaiming aloud, while the Union soldiers were in Darlington, "Bless the Lord, the Yankees have come!" While the local press, *The Darlington New Era* and *The Charleston Courier*, reported that Darlington citizens had banded together in an effort to reverse the death penalty decreed by a military court, the pro-abolition, New York-based *Harper's Weekly* regarded Amy Spain as, quite simply, a martyr to Southern racism. What none of these reports took into account, it seems, was the increasingly paranoid atmosphere that prevailed across the South as defeat loomed.[12] Mary Richards Bowser did not need to have heard the tragic story of Amy Spain to be fully aware of the risks she herself was running in acts so much more consequential than those of young Amy.

By April 1864, Varina Davis was convinced that "the fall of Richmond must come." She talked of sending her children away to stay with Mary Chesnut at her home in Camden, South Carolina. Chesnut begged Varina to come too, but Varina would not leave her husband's side.

By this stage, Jefferson Davis was constantly ill. His energy was drained by bouts of malaria, by facial neuralgia, indigestion, and migraines brought on by anxiety. He suffered acutely, too, from the mounting public criticism of his handling of the economy and the war. Varina wrote of this time:

> My husband's health was at this time very precarious, and he was too weak to ride to headquarters. General Lee came up from camp one day evidently worn out and worried, to find Mr. Davis lying quite ill on a divan, in a little morning-room in which we received only our intimate friends.

At the end of April, the household was plunged into mourning for five-year-old Joseph Evan, the Davises' favorite child, who on the 30th fell from a balcony at the mansion and died of his injuries shortly after. As Varina described it, the shock of this sudden tragedy left her husband too dazed to relate to the world around him:

> A courier came with a dispatch. He took it, held it open for some moments, and looked at me fixedly, saying, "Did you tell me what was in it?" I saw his mind was momentarily paralyzed by the blow, but at last he tried to write an answer, and then called out, in a heart-broken tone, "I must have this day with my little child." Somebody took the dispatch to General Cooper and left us alone with our dead.[13]

Davis paced up and down his room all through the night. Varina lay prostrate, scarcely able to speak to anyone. Did Mary feel pity for the bereaved president and his wife, crushed as they were by shock and grief? Or did she gloat over their misery—perhaps regarding their tragedy as God's revenge for their sins as slave owners? Poor Joseph Evan, though, had been innocent of any crime. Whether or not she pitied the family, Mary had a job to do, and feelings had to be set aside: there was more on her mind than the personal sorrows of others.

The gloom in the Davis household was somewhat relieved when Varina, two months after the death of her son, gave birth to a daughter, Varina Anne. Nothing, however, could obscure the fact that the Confederacy was in dire straits, both on the battlefront and at home. The economy was in free fall. By June 1864, the Confederate dollar, with no gold or hard currency to back it, was worth just four cents. "Cotton is five cents a pound," Mary Chesnut wrote in her diary, "and labor of no value at all; it commands no price whatever. People gladly hire out their negroes to have them fed and clothed...."[14]

That summer, when Mary Chesnut called on the Davis family, she found the household in a ferment of activity. All was bustle and confusion as messengers arrived at the house one after another with dispatches, and left with orders and instructions. Only now did Chesnut learn of the grim predicament of the Confederate forces:

> Calmly General Elzey discoursed upon our present weakness and our chances for aid. After a while Mrs. Davis came out and embraced me silently. "It is dreadful," I said. "The enemy is within forty miles of us—only forty!" "Who told you that tale?" said she. "They are within three miles of Richmond!" I went down on my knees like a stone. "You had better be quiet," she said. "The President is ill. Women and children

must not add to the trouble." She asked me to stay all night, which I was thankful to do.

The Union troops did not take Richmond on that occasion. The reprieve would last a whole eight months, even as Confederate forces across the South yielded one strategic point after another. It was obvious to anyone who thought about it, however, that the fighting was only prolonging the inevitable.

Again, Mary Chesnut, unlike most of her white fellow-citizens, found time to speculate on the thoughts and feelings of her enslaved black servants. In the summer of 1864, as their final liberation drew near, she reflected on the inscrutable manner of those who waited on her so obediently in her own home. They must, she wrote in her diary,

> know what is at hand.... "Freedom! my masters!" But these sphinxes give no sign, unless it be increased diligence and absolute silence, as certain in their action and as noiseless as a law of nature, at any rate when we are in the house.[15]

In Richmond, the end, when it came, was swift. While Jefferson Davis was at worship in St. Paul's Church near his residence on Sunday, April 2, 1865, a telegram was handed to him. It came from Robert E. Lee. In it, Lee announced his retreat from Petersburg. He could no longer protect Richmond from being overrun by Union troops.

Davis at once ordered the evacuation of the city. He and his family left Richmond that night, taking few possessions. Husband and wife split up for the journey, agreeing to meet again in Danville, 158 miles away, where Davis, with members of his cabinet, hoped to regroup his forces and begin to organize some kind of resistance. As Varina tells it:

> The day before our departure Mr. Davis gave me a pistol and showed me how to load, aim, and fire it. He was very apprehensive of our falling into the hands of the disorganized bands of troops roving about the country, and said, "You can at least, if reduced to the last extremity, force your assailants to kill you, but I charge you solemnly to leave when you hear the enemy are approaching."[16]

By nightfall, Richmond was under heavy bombardment. All around, the darkness was lit up by the glare of bursting shells. The ground shook with their thunder. Down by the James River, the city was ablaze; the retreating Confederate troops had set alight the dockside warehouses to prevent their valuable stores falling into Union hands. The air was full of the crackling of flames and sudden reports as burning roofs collapsed—thick with rolling black smoke and the sweet aroma of burning tobacco. Prisoners were brought out of their cells to be transported away from the city, some escaping in the confusion.[17] Everywhere were shouts and screams and the clatter of wheels and hooves as people rushed about in panic.[17]

The Mayo Bridge was locked in an immovable jam of carts and carriages, loaded up with frightened families and their goods. Alongside them, poorer people trudged, with nothing but their children and their small bundles. Carters flailed their whips, swearing and shouting. Troops on horseback yelled to civilians to get out of their way. Under cover of the confusion, former slaves merged in with the crowd, and joined the hordes struggling over the bridge. Back in town, those who had stayed behind grabbed whatever they could out of damaged buildings. There was looting everywhere—no one seemed able to stop it, or even to care.

At what had been the White House of the Confederacy, Mary O'Melia took charge. Davis's manservant, Robert, and Varina's new maid, Ellen Barnes, had left with the family. Other servants had been dismissed or had quietly taken freedom into their own hands.

On April 3, Union troops under General Godfrey Weitzel marched into Richmond at the head of his African-American troops, to be greeted rapturously by the city's black residents. He set up his headquarters in Jefferson Davis's former residence.

Mary had not seen Richmond on fire, nor the panicked flight from the city. She was not there to greet the triumphant arrival of the victorious army. Either because she was threatened with discovery, or because her presence in the Davis household was no longer needed, she had slipped away, out of Richmond, weeks before the city fell. Like so many before her, she had made her way to the safety of the Union lines. Her dangerous work was done.

At the time, perhaps only Thomas McNiven fully acknowledged what Mary had accomplished for the Union cause, and for her own enslaved people. Yet when General Ulysses S. Grant told Elizabeth Van Lew, "You have sent me the most valuable information received from Richmond during the war," his tribute was, indirectly, acknowledging the key contribution of Mary Richards Bowser.[18]

Telling It Slant

Tell all the truth but tell it slant.

—Emily Dickinson

In the fall of 1865, for the first time in her life, Mary found herself famous. She was invited to speak in New York about her wartime experiences as a secret agent. Advertised as a talk by a woman who had been "in the secret service of the government," her first lecture attracted a fascinated crowd.[1]

The African Methodist Episcopal church at Bridge Street, where she spoke with the blessing of the minister, was packed to capacity. Latecomers had to be turned away. In their eagerness to find a space, people forgot their manners, and according to a reporter from the *Brooklyn Daily Eagle*, in the stifling heat of the crowded room, "several white ladies could be seen applying their elbows right and left."

The meeting began with singing and prayer.

Mary shared a platform with Henry Ward Beecher, brother of the famous anti-slavery novelist Harriet Beecher Stowe, author of *Uncle Tom's Cabin*. The speakers were introduced by William Howard Day, a leading black educator and campaigner for civil rights and an important figure in black liberation circles. In his introduction, Day described Mary as having done as much good in the world "as Florence Nightingale."

Mary brought with her witness statements in support of her claim to have been a spy for the Union. They were letters of recommendation from three high-ranking military men who had led troops in Virginia: Colonel Samuel H. Roberts, who had commanded troops in the Army of the James; General Alfred Terry, a well known war hero; and General Edward

Imaginary portrait of Mary
Richards by an unknown
artist. (*Courtesy of American
Battlefield Trust*)

Elizabeth Van Lew. (*Courtesy of
Virginia Historical Society*)

The Van Lew mansion, Church Hill, Richmond, in 1906. (*Virginia Commonwealth Libraries*)

The St. John's Episcopal church in Richmond, 1891. This is where Mary Richards was baptized and later married. (*Courtesy of British Library*)

Betsey Stockton,
c. 1863. (*Courtesy
of Hawaiian Mission
Houses Historic Site
and Archives*)

Joseph J. Roberts,
president of Liberia.
(*Library of Congress*)

Jefferson Davis in 1859. Portrait by
Matthew Brady. (*Library of Congress*)

Varina Howell Davis in 1860.
(*Courtesy of Civil War Museum,
Richmond*)

Above: The White House
of the Confederacy, *c.* 1904.
(*Courtesy of Virginia Department
of Historic Resources*)

Right: Female figure on the
Emancipation and Freedom
Monument, Richmond, 2021,
holding an emancipation document.
(*Wikimedia Commons*)

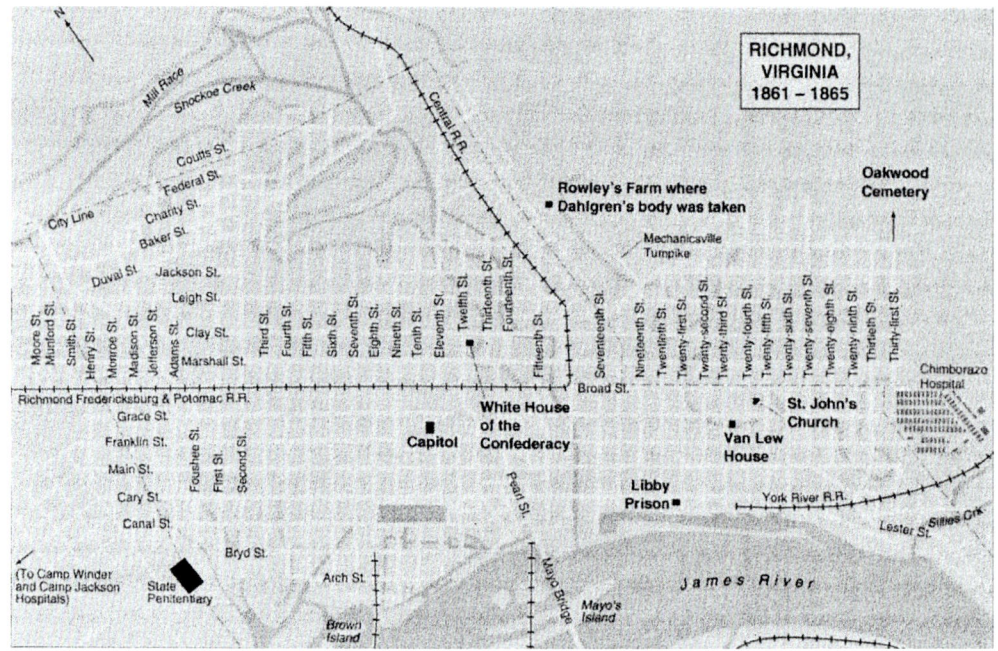

Richmond in 1863, showing key locations during the Civil War. (*Library of Congress*)

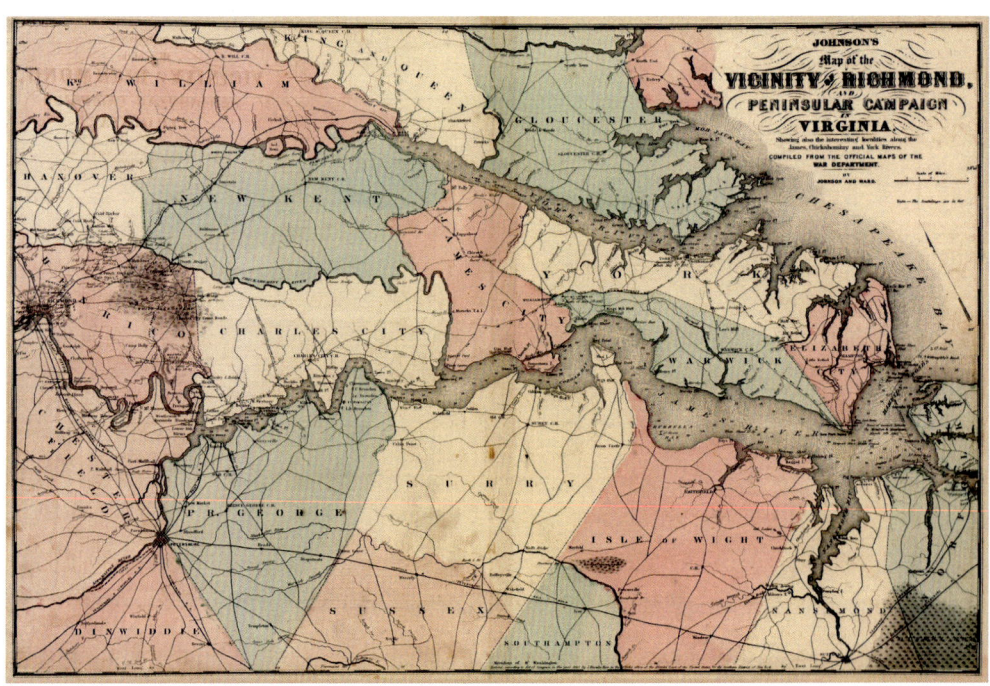

Civil War map: the Peninsula Campaign in Virginia, *c.* 1862. (*Library of Congress*)

Major General Ulysses S. Grant in 1865. (*Missouri History Museum*)

General Edward Ord in the White House of the Confederacy after the war. (*Courtesy of American Battlefield Trust*)

Left: Harriet Beecher Stowe, *c.* 1870. (*Library of Congress*)

Below: A Freedmen's Bureau agent intervenes in a conflict between freedmen and white farmers. Drawing by Alfred R. Waud for *Harper's Weekly*, 1868. (*Library of Congress*)

Ord, who had been overall commander of the Army of the James and had accepted the surrender of Robert E. Lee.

Professor Day introduced Mary as "Richmonia St. Pierre," a pseudonym to protect her from possible reprisals by Confederate sympathizers. Though she never again used the surname St. Pierre, she would continue to call herself Richmonia. Of all the names she was given in her life, she must have felt this was one, chosen by herself, that she could really claim as her own. From now on, she would be Mary Jane Richmonia Richards.

One name she had left behind for good, and would never use again, was that of Bowser. No details are known about Mary's relationship with Wilson Bowser, or what became of him after their marriage. What is known, however, is that after she began her work in the Davis mansion, he seems to have faded out of her life.

Mary said she was about to tell "a few plain facts" about herself, and to describe "how many changes a young and unprotected female might have to go through" on her journey through life. She claimed, at this point, to be "quite alone in the world." (Had she quarreled with Elizabeth Van Lew?)

She told the audience something of her experiences before the war: her upbringing in Virginia; her schooling in the North; her time in Liberia. (The *Eagle* report gives her time in Africa as six years, rather than the actual four, which was presumably the reporter's mistake.) Mary told of her despair, upon her return to America, at observing the apparent early success of the Confederacy, with its implications for the continuation of the slave system. Telling of the pass laws imposed on black people and the bans on assemblies, she impressed upon her audience the oppressive legal structures of slavery. She told, too, of the cruel and negligent treatment of Union prisoners of war, of the wounded Union soldiers brought into Richmond by the wagonload and thrown down on the sidewalks. Later in her address, she alluded to the brutality of Heinrich (Henry) Wirz, governor of the notorious Confederate military prison at Andersonville, Georgia, where over a quarter of the prisoners had died of abuse or neglect. (At the time of Richards' talk, Wirz was on trial for his crimes. He would be found guilty, and sentenced to death.)

The Confederate president had been well aware of conditions at Andersonville, Richards said:

She had heard expressions from the lips of Jefferson Davis which entirely condemned him. And not only he, but Memminger and Stephens, and General Lee, too, knew all about it. She advised government not to be so long about trying these men, as they get delicate during the operation, and recline in Court on sofas; and have to be fanned and other attentions paid to them. She wanted the work short and sure.

It could fairly be said that Richards was speaking before a sympathetic audience of admirers and friends—one made up predominantly of African Americans, with a minority of liberal-minded white people. All the same, mindful of the possibility of there being hostile listeners in the audience, she was careful of what she told her audience, editing some details of her story and altering others. She told them that on her return from Africa she had gone south, and lived "in the Confederacy four years in the guise of a slave." But she omitted to mention that her time posing as a slave had been spent in the Davis household; nor did she mention Elizabeth Van Lew or any other agents by name. Anyone familiar with Mary's story, though, can recognize the identity of the "delicate Southern lady, rich, well-known in the Confederacy," who lived in "a splendid white mansion" somewhere in Richmond. Shabbily dressed—"as a beggar," Mary told her audience—this lady had taken Mary with her on her visits to the prisons where captured Union soldiers were held:

> "Why, cousin John," [Van Lew] would say, addressing one of the prisoners, the Confederate guard looking on meanwhile ... "Why, Mr. So and So, how came you to get in the Union army? I am ashamed of you!"

The audience laughed and applauded.

The lady in her mansion, Mary said, "was suspected of being a spy," but "left unharmed, as no proof could be found against her."

Mary described Jefferson Davis's suspicions and anxieties about the presence of Union agents in Richmond, but mentioned nothing more about him in connection to her own activities. She omitted any mention of Thomas McNiven or Christopher Taylor, of their bakery, or almost any of the specific intelligence she herself obtained, or how she came by it. Anyone hoping for such details might well have been disappointed, but she had others to protect beside herself.

We do learn a little from this talk about Mary's activities in Virginia towards the end of the war. She "escaped" from Richmond, she said, before the fall of the Confederacy. She then spent time in Norfolk, teaching former slaves with the newly established New England Freedmen's Aid Society, before going back to Richmond after the city's capture by federal troops and working there as a teacher with the American Missionary Society. In Richmond, she was debriefed by the provost marshal, the military official responsible for policing in the city, to whom she gave "a good deal of information on certain subjects which [the] government wanted to possess." Again, she remained cautious, saying only that she "was taken into the confidence of the government."

Towards the end of her speech, Mary described incidents of racism experienced by herself and others from quarters where it might be least expected. At the New England Freedmen's Aid Society, she said she was "not treated with anything like the proper consideration," owing, she believed, to the darkness of her complexion. She spoke in general terms of similar experiences in the North, where, despite much liberal talk about the evils of slavery, it might happen that if "a colored man or woman calls at the houses of ... Abolitionists, they are not 'at home' to them." She went on to describe a shocking incident in Richmond, where a Union general, at the time provost marshal of the Henrico District (and possibly the same man who had interviewed Mary earlier), had ordered the execution of a black man who got into a fight with a white man while defending his wife from being shoved and insulted on the street. General Marsena Patrick had ordered the black man to be made an example of. He was smeared with molasses to attract insects and put out in the sun to be jeered at and insulted, after which he was to be shot; had someone not appealed to President Johnson who intervened to save his life.

Mary ended her talk by calling on everyone who could, to go to the South to teach and otherwise support newly freed Southern blacks— "not to talk sympathy so much," she said, with more than an edge of sarcasm, "but to do something for their colored brothers and sisters." And she called for the right to vote. In the war, black people had fought with bayonets for their freedom—now they must have the ballot. But she was "half afraid that Northern Abolitionists would do nothing more than talk, and that the colored race would not obtain justice." She warned of the interracial violence that could ensue if black people's rights were denied them—"insurrection worse than anything" that had "yet taken place." "Do us justice," Mary concluded, "Or I say, Look out, look out!"

A collection was taken up to support Mary's educational work in the South. She would return to that work, it was said, once her health had "become sufficiently re-established." The illness that had brought her home from Liberia was possibly still taking its toll on her energy.

If Mary complained of racist attitudes among those who might have been expected to know better, she could not have been entirely pleased by the manner in which the journalist from the *Brooklyn Daily Eagle* reported her speech. If not directly racist, it certainly is often condescending, beginning with the reporter's description of "Miss St. Pierre." After calling Mary "a good looking young woman of six and twenty," and comparing her "in height and general appearance," and in "fire and vim," to the white abolitionist campaigner Anna Dickinson, he added that Mary wholly lacked Dickinson's "cultivation and polish."

The description of the audience at one point has racist overtones, as the reporter related how, in the general overcrowding of the meeting, white women only managed to find seats "wedged firmly in between some lusty specimens of male Blacks." When Mary gave her account of General Patrick's cruelty in Richmond—a story that clearly followed on from what she had just said about her own experience of racism in unexpected quarters—the reporter implied that her narrative was disjointed and illogical. She supposedly "went off at a tangent" and "pitched into" General Patrick. Her closing words of warning about violence if black people were denied the vote, were, he claimed, "almost unintelligible in the excitement into which she had worked herself." (They were intelligible enough for him to take them down verbatim.) Although the reporter supplied his readers with some useful facts, the portrait he gave of Mary as an individual—uncultivated, irrational, and at one point almost hysterical—is scarcely a flattering one.

The lecture Richards gave two weeks earlier, at New York's Abyssinian Baptist church, was more favorably reported by a black newspaper, *The Anglo-African*. As in the Bridge Street church, Mary spoke to what the reporter described as "a large intelligent and appreciative audience."[2] As for the talk at the African Methodist Episcopal church, black people here were in the majority. Again, Mary was largely preaching to the converted.

The write-up of this event in *The Anglo-African* differs markedly from that of the previous talk in the *Brooklyn Daily Eagle*. Where the *Eagle* reporter saw irrelevant digressions and incoherent, near-hysterical emotion in Mary's delivery, the *Anglo-African* reporter describes a woman in command of her narrative, and of herself. "Throughout the delivery of her speech she was very sarcastic and at times quite humorous," he wrote. But some of what is reported about "Richmonia Richards" in this account is both puzzling and intriguing, raising more questions than it answers about Mary's family connections and her activities during and after the Civil War.

Interestingly, although she still called herself Richmonia rather than Mary, on this occasion she went by her own surname of Richards. She gave her audience a similar account of her early years to that in the Bridge Street church, up to the time of her journey to Liberia. Whether or not she gave details about Liberia in the other talk that the *Brooklyn Daily Eagle* reporter did not bother to include, we shall never know. In this case, however, and in spite of the illness she contracted in Africa, she was at pains to assure her audience that the Liberian climate was not especially hostile, but much like that of any other tropical country. The land was immensely fertile, she added, with rich soil and abundant crops and vegetation. She appreciated, too, some aspects of the local culture in a way wholly alien to the attitudes of many of her fellow emigrants. As the *Anglo-African* paraphrased it, "The inhabitants are much better than the colored people here. There is one tribe of the Mendingoes who never drink, lie, nor steal, and have a religion based upon those principles." (The Mandingo people in Liberia were, and are, predominantly Muslim.)

However "normal" the Liberian climate might be for a tropical region, Mary all the same had to admit to her audience that the same climate had made her ill enough to compel her to return to America. There, she said, "her foster-sister, a Miss A," had invited her to "visit the former home of her childhood."

Who is this "foster-sister?" Is she talking about Elizabeth's cousin Anna Whitlock? Or is she referring to some member of the Richards branch of the Van Lew family? Does Miss A. actually exist? Almost certainly yes, or why would Mary bother to name a "Miss A" at all? But why would she have to wait to "be invited" to her former home—presumably the Van Lew mansion? Did she have to be persuaded to go back to Elizabeth, her time in Liberia having ended in disgrace? Or is she once again spinning a story to distract attention from her connection with the Van Lews?

The *Anglo-African* gave an account of Mary's arrest in Richmond for being out without a pass. According to the newspaper report, the arresting watchman took her to the lockup, where the following morning she "received five lashes." She was then, we are told, "sold into slavery" (something we know never happened). Did the *Anglo-African* reporter simply get the facts wrong? Was Mary romancing at this point—adding a little more drama to her story than was strictly necessary? Or possibly she needed a way to explain how she came to be regarded as a slave in her undercover work during the war without mentioning either her time in the Jefferson Davis household, or implicating Van Lew as coordinator of the Richmond spy ring.

While "in servitude," Richards then told her audience, she was recruited into something she called "the Union League in Richmond," and through that connection "performed many important secret services for the Union cause":

> She clandestinely entered in the Rebel Senate while in secret session, considering the sweeping Conscription bill which included in its provisions every male capable of carrying a gun, no matter how young, or how old. Immediately on its passage through the Senate Miss R. communicated the fact to the Union League.

Richards seems to be referring to the Third Conscription Act, passed on February 17, 1864, which provided for the conscription of white males aged between seventeen and fifty, for the duration of the war. While such an action is not impossible, it is more likely that she learned about the conscription bill through some conversation overheard in the home of Jefferson Davis. As on other occasions, Mary was carefully covering her tracks.

As in previous statements, she refrained from saying directly that she had worked for the Davis family. Instead, she told an improbable story:

> She went into President Davis's house while he was absent, seeking for washing, and while there was conducted into a private office by one of the clerks, when she opened the drawers of a cabinet and scrutinized the papers. While thus employed Jeff came in and inquired of her what she was doing there, but considering she was colored, allowed her to go in peace.

If she went to the house "seeking for washing"—perhaps pretending to be a poor woman asking for an odd job doing laundry—why would anyone show her to a "private office"? During her time in the Davis household, Mary might indeed have been surprised in the president's office, looking at paperwork she was not supposed to see. But it would have been when she was working in the house; or possibly at night, after the family and other servants had gone to bed. And, as she herself implied, if caught there her safeguard would have been her lowly status as a black woman, presumed to be illiterate. Again, the story seems invented to cover her tracks.

The next point in Mary's story presents us with a tantalizing gap in our knowledge of her activities in the final year of the war. "Last fall," she told her audience—that is, late in 1864, roughly four or five months before the Davises' hasty departure and the entry into Richmond of the victorious Union troops—she left Richmond and went to Fredericksburg. At first glance, this seems quite likely; many fugitive blacks took advantage of an end-of-year lull in the fighting that intermittently raged around the contested city, to make their way out of Richmond. Mary could well have joined them.

In Fredericksburg, she told her audience, according to the *Anglo-African*, "she aided in capturing a large amount of tobacco, and two Confederate officers." It would be interesting to know how she assisted the capture—possibly it was simply by telling the military what she knew. It seems unlikely that she physically took part in a raid, although at least one other black woman agent, Harriet Tubman, is known to have done so.

Richards went on to tell of General Patrick's cruelty to the black man who defended his wife; the same anecdote that appeared in the *Brooklyn Daily Eagle* report. Clearly, it was a story that moved her deeply, impressing upon her the flagrant hypocrisy of certain white people who claimed to care about the oppression of blacks.

The *Anglo-African* noted Richards' passionate concern for the empowerment, rights, and progress of her people, and reported that she ended her speech by "advising our young ladies and gentlemen not to bury their talents which were so bounteously given them" in an obsession with dress and fashion. Her statement on this subject is quoted in the paper in full:

> Too much attention is given to the style of your dress or your bonnet, which I have learned from experience is the only condition of admission to social circles here. Young ladies and young gentlemen, turn your attention to the education and the adornment of your minds rather than your persons, which are to be the great lever of our elevation as a people.

Mary practiced what she preached. Passionate about education and the "elevation" of her people, and moved by all the missionary fervor of her religious upbringing, she left New York and returned to the South, to carry on her work as a teacher.

Teacher to the Free

*We soon found out that freedom could make folks proud but it
didn't make them rich.*

—Former slave Felix Haywood, interviewed in
San Antonio, Texas, at the age of ninety-two

Many former slaves who dreamed their liberation would bring about a
golden age of peace and plenty, were to be bitterly disappointed by the
realities of Reconstruction in the South. This was especially true of those
freed people, the rural majority, whose lot had been to toil and suffer
on the great plantations that had generated the wealth of the Southern
states. They had hoped for land to call their own, and an opportunity to
make it prosper for the benefit of themselves and their families. For some,
freedom from slavery offered the chance to move away—to the North, or
even simply to a nearby town, to make a different kind of life from the
endless drudgery they had known as slaves. These choices brought their
own challenges. But for many who had little choice but to stay on the
land, freedom was merely a new kind of servitude.

In lands devastated by the war, where opportunities beyond agriculture
were few for those without education, and often limited by the racist
attitudes of white people, many former slaves found themselves still bound
to carry on toiling on the plantation. They were wage earners now, but so
meagerly paid that their labor was a form of slavery. If they rented a patch
of land, they could end up in hock to the landowner, who advanced them
tools and seeds in return for a portion of the crop. When the crop failed,
they fell deeper and deeper into debt, so that they were tied to the land

just as before. Those who were more fortunate could be assigned part of a white planter's confiscated estate by the federal government, though it was usually the least productive part. They might manage to scratch out a living from the unyielding soil, but always in the hostile shadow of their white neighbors.

In hopes of a better life for themselves and their children, many freed people put their faith in the gift that had been denied them as slaves—that of gaining an education, starting with learning to read and write.

White people in Georgia in 1865 had grievances of their own, and good reasons for hating the U.S. government. General Sherman's euphemistically named "March to the Sea" had been a scorched-earth strategy designed to crush and intimidate the white Southern population, and deter all thought of any further resistance to federal rule. "We are not only fighting armies," Sherman wrote to General Henry Halleck in justification of his ruthless methods, "but a hostile people, and must make old and young, rich and poor, feel the hard hand of war, as well as their organized armies." He wanted the beaten population not only to know of their defeat theoretically, but to experience it in the harshest terms in their own lives:

> I know that this recent movement of mine through Georgia has had a wonderful effect in this respect. Thousands who had been deceived by their lying papers into the belief that we were being whipped all the time, realized the truth, and have no appetite for a repetition of the same experience.[1]

From November to December 1864, Sherman's army marched across Georgia from Augusta in the west to the port of Savannah in the east, burning and wrecking as they went. In a bid to crush any remaining resistance to the Union forces, they set fire to farms and warehouses, and destroyed railroads and mills. In the spring, the same treatment was visited on the Carolinas. It left a trail of devastation across the South— miles of burned-out houses with grieving and starving families. There were many reports of killings, rapes, and other—some perhaps exaggerated— atrocities. Other crimes were committed not by the regular Union troops but by so-called "bushwhackers," hangers-on to the main army who were motivated mainly by a desire to plunder.

Mary Chesnut wrote of the devastation she witnessed in South Carolina:

> Columbia is but dust and ashes, burned to the ground. Men, women, and children have been left there homeless, and without one particle of food—reduced to picking up corn that was left by Sherman's horses on picket grounds and parching it to stay their hunger…. Since we left

Chester nothing but solitude, nothing but tall blackened chimneys, to show that any man has ever trod this road before. This is Sherman's track. It is hard not to curse him.[2]

The war-ravaged communities across the South, with their stark memorials of abandoned mill chimneys left standing on sites where prosperous industries had been, were now home to resentful and bitter white people. They regarded the military administrators sent to implement the reconstruction of their communities less as agents of their national government, than as foreign overlords, the representatives of an alien power.

It was into this shattered world that idealistic people like Mary Richards arrived to support the educational work of the newly founded Bureau of Refugees, Freedmen and Abandoned Lands, also known as the Freedmen's Bureau.

The bureau had been set up in 1865 under the presidency of Abraham Lincoln to distribute "provisions, clothing, and fuel for the immediate and temporary shelter and supply of destitute and suffering refugees and freedmen and their wives and children." Its remit quickly grew to cover more than immediate humanitarian relief, such as the supply of food and medical treatment and aid to black veterans. The new agency began tracing missing persons, reuniting families torn apart by slavery and war, mediating disputes between white and black residents of Southern communities, helping negotiate labor contracts between white employers and their newly freed slaves. In conjunction with the American Missionary Association and other philanthropic organizations and individuals, it oversaw the founding of thousands of schools. From this pioneering educational project would come a modest increase in black literacy.

In many cases, the bureau merely offered support to educational work already being undertaken by African Americans themselves. Out of these efforts by pioneering black people—and, it would seem, totally against the odds given the scarcity of material resources after the war—the great African-American universities of the South were established: Howard, Fisk, Atlanta, and Hampton, all of which still exist today.

In August 1865, Reverend Jermain Loguen, the well-known abolitionist, wrote a passionate appeal to Northern blacks to teach in the new schools for freed former slaves:

It is necessary that we urge every strong man and woman, preacher and teacher, who can leave for a time their Northern laboring fields, to go and spend all the time they can in the South. Let them stay two, three, or more months, just as they can afford. The work must be done, and it is for us who have had the advantages of a free North and free schools....[3]

The Freedmen's Bureau was never adequately staffed or funded. At the height of its operations, it employed no more than 900 agents at most, spread thinly over the whole of the South. Nor were these agents always keen advocates for the freed people. Many came from military backgrounds, and viewed their role mainly as that of policemen, with the emphasis on keeping the former slaves from "getting above themselves" or "getting out of hand." They saw their job as damping down what were sometimes considered excessively "radical" aspirations among blacks—such as demands for political equality with white people. Then there were Northerners who viewed their role almost literally as that of missionaries—converting former slaves from their supposedly backward customs such as their allegedly easy-going attitudes to relations between the sexes, and even their eating habits. Freedmen must "be taught to respect the marriage-vow," wrote John Bryant, the first bureau agent to serve in rural Georgia, and to abandon what he called the "barbarous habit" of "eating hominy from the pot in which it is cooked."[4]

When Richmond surrendered to the Union troops, Mary Richards had been employed there for a time by the Baptist Home Mission Society. The society funded a school in the First African Baptist church, conveniently close to the Van Lews' house on Church Hill. That position gave Mary a base from which to work. She would teach continuously thereafter, setting up new schools in Virginia where none had existed before. As she said herself, after the war she was responsible for starting "some of the first schools in Richmond" for freed slaves.[5] She began to question the usefulness of staying in Richmond, however, when the need was clearly so much greater further south. (By 1867, Virginia had seventy-eight schools for freed people, mainly in Richmond, while the entire state of Georgia had only seven.)[6] Mary, as a protégée of Elizabeth Van Lew, imbued with the Van Lew ethos of public service, was never one to take the easiest option. She moved out of Virginia to teach in Florida, then in Georgia.

Even in rural Georgia, where schools were so few, the appetite for education among the black population was strong. In fact, wherever education was offered across the South, freed people, adults, and children alike, flocked to the classroom. Meetings were held to form school boards and associations, and teachers were sought who might be willing to work in impoverished rural communities for meager pay. Almost anyone, it seemed, could step forward to start a school and apply for funding from the Freedmen's Bureau.

Not all white Southerners were hostile to the idea of the education of former slaves. Some positively welcomed it. To the more liberal minded, it seemed important to demonstrate to racists in the white community that blacks could live peaceful, law-abiding lives alongside their neighbors, and make valuable contributions to society. In a letter to Major Gilbert Eberhart, Georgia's superintendent for education at the Freedmen's Bureau, one J. H. Caldwell—possibly himself a bureau employee—called for increased recruitment of teachers for the freedmen schools. "Everyone of these we can fit," he wrote, "will help in the great work of reconstruction by breaking down the walls of prejudice among their friends." Caldwell was particularly keen to see the appointment of young Southerners as role models to their fellow citizens.

Even ex-slave owners might join in the projects for freed people's education. In Georgia's Lee and Dougherty counties, a Mr. Lee and a Mr. Jordan, owners of seven plantations between them, decided to club together to build a schoolhouse and start a school for their former slaves.

The motives for this kind of support were mixed. In Macon, Georgia, another plantation owner offered to meet the entire cost of starting a school for his 175 black laborers in order to set an example to his neighbors, but also, as he put it, "to surround myself with a better class of tenants." He wanted to hire a teacher, but would not employ anyone who engaged in "preaching politics." (Interestingly, this landowner knew of the school Mary Richards had founded in St. Marys, 2 miles from his plantation, but he wanted one nearer his home.)

A doctor named Hansen wrote to the bureau from Jefferson County, offering to raise funds to establish a school in his area. In his letter, dated May 23, 1867, he wrote of the "hundreds of bright-eyed, smart little darkies" in his area, "who must become educated and useful citizens of the country, or they will relapse into barbarism, and become a curse to themselves and the country." The children and their parents were, he conceded, "all athirst for knowledge."

Given the enthusiasm of both students and their teachers, there were almost guaranteed to be inspiring successes in spite of practical difficulties. As one teacher reported proudly to the bureau on June 13, 1867, white visitors to a school in Americus, Georgia, seemed to be "perpetually astonished at the improvement of the children" since their education had begun. The neighbors were so impressed that they donated a house for the school's use. In July, the students "were thoroughly examined by several white men," who were said to be equally impressed by the pupils' achievements.

Mary was not alone in her sense of mission—of duty. There were plenty of people interested in founding, and funding, new "freedmen" schools. Willing, idealistic teachers were not lacking, either. Indeed, anyone who came forward to teach former slaves had to be motivated by something other than ambition to climb the career ladder. In addition to the low pay, primitive conditions, and lack of basic teaching materials, many of the schools were isolated from city amenities and attracted the hostility of white neighbors. Prospective teachers had to be extremely dedicated.

Teachers, all the same, came from near and far. There were young, fresh college graduates from the North, retired and practicing missionaries—both white and black—and committed black Southerners like Mary Richards. Some of these educators had teaching experience, and some nothing to offer but their enthusiasm. There were even a few people from professions other than teaching; for example, a surgeon—"a man of superior education," according to an acquaintance—offered his services to the Freedmen's Bureau, in a letter of May 28.

As a Southern-born black woman, Mary was in a minority. Black teachers were predominantly male, while female instructors were mainly white and from the North. Given the challenges of the job and the social expectations of women in the nineteenth century, it is not surprising that male teachers outnumbered women two to one.[7]

As the full title of the Freedmen's Bureau suggests, its remit went well beyond providing education. In fact, for an organization staffed by bureaucrats and former military officers, and tasked with redistributing land, tracing missing persons, and resettling refugees, education seems to have been a fairly low priority at times. But the bureau did oversee the work of schools, and occasionally manage to fund them, though not without the requirement of a great deal of paperwork: endless reports and form filling to check that funds were being appropriately used.

The little town of St. Marys, where Mary Richards went to set up her new school, is in Georgia's Camden County. It was largely in ruins when Mary arrived. The war-decimated population there totaled about 700. The nearest town of any size was Savannah, 110 miles away. St. Marys lies 6 miles from the Atlantic, and 40 from Jacksonville, Florida, across the St. Marys River. The area is bordered along the coast by miles of mudflats and swamp, and veined with winding streams and creeks. When Mary first arrived, it was February, the weather cool and mild. By mid-summer, the temperature would climb into the nineties, with moist air and frequent heavy rain. It must have reminded her of Liberia.

The cultural and geographical isolation of the town of St. Marys is shown by the gratitude with which Mary wrote in June 1867 to Gilbert Eberhart, the education superintendent, for sending her newspapers: "I was very much obliged to you ..." she told him. "They were quite a treat, as reading matter is very scarce down here."

Plenty of books were available for students in the new schools—if a school could afford them. The white Congregationalists of the American Tract Society had commissioned specially designed texts for the education of freed slaves. *The Freedman's Primer* and *The Freedman's Spelling*

Book, along with *The Lincoln Primer*, were designed to get the student started on the way to literacy. Once basic reading ability was acquired, students could, with growing confidence, develop and maintain their skills by working through a series of three more advanced "Freedman's Readers." While designed to teach reading and writing, the books were also unashamedly propagandist. Their secondary aim was to "civilize" the allegedly uncivilized freed people—meaning to coach them in humble submission and respect for "betters"—along with honesty, thrift, and piety. Robert Hamilton, editor of *The Anglo-African*, a perceptive African-American commentator, spoke out against such demeaning attitudes: "There is a type of education, which, if introduced at the South, will train our race in mental subserviency for fifty years to come." This, he wrote, "would be a disaster. It would be exchanging physical for intellectual bondage." There should be no teaching, he went on, "which will train the freed people to regard themselves as an inferior race." One insurance against such indoctrination would be the role to be played by black educators: "The field is appropriately ours—it is the only fair scope we ever had for usefulness before."[8]

Not all textbooks had a racist ideological subtext. Texts like Fetter's *Primary Arithmetic*, Goodrich's *Pictorial History of the United States*, Montieth's *United States History*, and Webster's *Speller* were widely used and had a more neutral, or at least less overtly biased agenda.

A perennial complaint of the teachers whose work was overseen by the Freedmen's Bureau was about money. Local people were supposed to contribute to the upkeep of schools, including the teacher's salary, but in spite of the obvious thirst for education, black communities often struggled to feed and clothe themselves and lacked the means to pay for education.

A federal bureau agent in Georgia wrote to his superiors in May 1867 about one school that had been up and running for a month. The local people were eager to have the school, but were desperately poor, and found even the sum of $1 per head per month beyond their means. The agent, a Mr. Davenport, appealed to the bureau: Owing to "the scarcity of means and the prevailing destitution," he wrote, "they will be obliged to forego the privilege of schooling unless the Govt renders some assistance."

Whether Davenport's appeal for funding was successful is unknown. Gilbert Eberhart, the superintendent of education, believed that freed people should pay for education themselves as a way of teaching self-reliance, and giving them independence.[9] But in any case, there was never enough money to meet the need for schooling for everyone, and what the federal government offered former slaves was, at best, a token gesture. It has been estimated that, as Davenport confirmed in a report of May 13,

1867, the freedmen schools in that year were reaching no more than 10 percent of freed blacks, and the simplest needs were often unobtainable. In April 1867, Eberhart received a letter from a Mr. Simon Beard, requesting "a Bible for a church out in the country that has none." Even something as basic and essential as a Bible for a parish church had become unaffordable.

Finding a suitable schoolhouse could also be an issue. The local black church might provide a space, but a rainproof barn with a dirt floor, or a spare room in someone's house was often the best a teacher could hope for. And when pupils and their families proved unable to support them, teachers often worked without pay. In February 1869, a teacher named Hettie Sabattie, based in Darien, 50 miles to the north of St. Marys, along the same stretch of coast, wrote to J. Murray Hoag, an assistant superintendent at the bureau:

> You will please if it is convenient let me know something about my pay for the time that I had the school here, as I am much in want of means.... I took the school on the first of January and kept it until the other teachers came and not one person ever gave me a cent.

Mary encountered similar problems. In June 1867, she found herself writing to Gilbert Eberhart, asking the bureau to supplement the payment she received from the local people. She sometimes got a mere $10 from them for salary, she told him, and sometimes only five. In January and February, she had received nothing at all:

> I have been here five months and all they could collect in that time has been fifteen dollars, about one month and a half's pay. The people here work hard but they don't make much money.

Mary pointed out that teachers in freedmen schools normally were paid $47, broken down as $20 for salary and $27 for board and lodging, "and in places where it is not half as hard to live as it is in this place." Mary's school was truly in a pioneering outpost, desperately poor, cut off from the bigger towns, and almost, it seems, from the outside world. Still, "I have not been paid" was a perennial complaint in letters to the Freedmen's Bureau. If Mary suspected that other teachers shared her difficulties, though, it can hardly have been much consolation to think that others were struggling just as she was.

Hers was pioneering work, but in her first letter to her new employers in Georgia, dated February 22, 1867, she indicated that she felt herself to be in something of a false situation: "I take the liberty to write to you sir to define to you my position here as teacher of the Freedmen School."

Why was her position in need of "defining"? Was her presence in St Marys not welcome? Was she suspected of taking someone else's job? But Superintendent Eberhart had written to his Florida counterpart about Mary Richards, at that time employed in the neighboring state, and Richards had been advised to contact Eberhart directly about her wish to start the school at St Marys. So what was the problem? The position, in this isolated, war-ravaged community, was, as Mary herself pointed out in her letter, unlikely to be a coveted one: "I did not wish to force myself upon the Board as a teacher," she insisted, "but it seemed as if no one was willing to be the first to come here for that purpose." She was offering to undertake work no one else wanted:

> I expected to have taken charge of a school on a plantation at the South end of Amelia Island, and was to have gone to that place the first of January, but before I had made up my mind Mr. Emerson the Supt Bd Ed Fla [Superintendent of the Board of Education for Florida] ... told me that a school was much more needed over here, and he thought that the people here would be able to pay something, and that in all probability the Gov would help support the school, if anyone would start it, he also explained that there was no school for freedmen here in the vicinity. I then determined to come here and try.

She was at pains to impress the Freedmen's Bureau with her commitment, and her willingness to work hard in her new post:

> I arrived here on Friday. I opened a day school on the following Monday without any prospect of where I was to get even money to continue to pay my board. I taught two weeks ... from the first day I commenced I have been teaching regularly taking charge even of the Sunday school, in the day school I would never wish for an assistant.

Mary was, of course, no stranger to teaching by now. As she wrote proudly in her letter to the Freedmen's Bureau dated February 22, 1867, it had "always been her lot" to "organize and teach the first term" in any newly founded school. Now she had begun teaching, she had found that although the black community at St. Marys were "anxious for the school," they were "perfectly unable to pay for the schooling of their children." However, she reiterated her willingness to take on the challenge: "I felt that I had the Advantage over the most of my race both in Blood and Intelligence, and that it was my duty if possible to work where I was most needed." She had been supported in her resolution to stay and teach in St. Marys by a local surgeon, Dr. Augustus Mitchell, who had assured her that her school would "certainly be protected, and in all probability supported."

The bureau's response to Mary's indirect request for funding was encouraging, if not backed up by an actual grant of money. She was relieved when at last the bureau saw fit to issue her with "blanks"—the report forms that teachers working under the bureau's auspices were required to fill out and submit monthly. The blanks amounted to an official stamp of approval for her position at St. Marys, and were a good start, allowing her "to feel more settled." She wrote to Eberhart that she would now go on with her work "more heartily than before," adding enthusiastically, "I need Books, Spellers, First Readers, and about four Second Readers, one dozen copy Books, eight Geographies ... Slates ... Primary Mathematics, I want a Blackboard very much." These materials were in addition to a writing desk she'd had made at her own expense.

On March 10, Mary wrote again to the Freedmen's Bureau, this time to acknowledge her receipt of money—$40. Whether this was for an advance on salary or was money to buy school supplies, she did not say, but it was another encouraging sign of support. "I am truly grateful to you for so soon acknowledging my letters," she wrote to Eberhart. "I cannot tell you how much better I feel than I did a week ago." She went on to assure him that the school was "improving very much indeed," and she noted, "I am glad to hear that you are going to send me some books."

Mary had been working tirelessly. In the space of just a month, she had gathered together a large class with "regular attendance of more than fifty children." She taught twenty girls sewing every Friday, and also had them "go over the commandments and catechism."

Religious instruction was central to the school's program, and it would have been welcomed by her students and their families. For so long these devout Christians had been denied access to the written word; a pressing motive for many freed former slaves to enroll in literacy classes was to learn how to read the Bible. They also wanted their children to have an early introduction to the Word. The number of students in the "sabbath school," Mary told Eberhart, was seventy-five.

Running the school at St. Marys was always going to be an enormous challenge, not least because Mary was completely on her own. "I have to act superintendent and teacher also, as there is no one to help me," she wrote. She confessed to Eberhart that occasionally self-doubt rose up within her:

I am I hope willing to do what I can but I fear that in the end it will not prove much. The colored people here are not of the best type of freedmen. A teacher has much to do, to really fill the situation deservingly and conscientiously. I sometimes feel that I have not the ability, to do all I see and feel to be my duty, but rest assured sir I will try to do my best, by the help of God.

Though anxious to convince Eberhart she was up to the job, Mary still could not refrain from admitting how she struggled at times with her task. One has to wonder whether it was wise for her to be so honest to a potentially critical superior. Writing on March 10, she hastened to tell Eberhart of the encouragement she had just received from a distinguished visitor:

> Mr. Kennedy corresponding secretary of the New York Freedmen's Union commission, called to see me yesterday, he gave me a great deal of encouragement, and I feel much more like going forward and trying to continue to do my best....

The Reverend Crammond Kennedy was a man well known in educational circles as a fervent supporter of the education of freed former slaves. He would later give his own account of this visit to Mary Richards' school in a letter to *The American Freedman*: "We stopped at St. Marys, Georgia, and found a young colored woman, Miss J. R. R. Richards, who teaches about seventy day-scholars, a dozen adults in the evening, and nearly a hundred children on Sundays."

For several years, Kennedy had been busy traveling to raise funds for schools such as the one in St. Marys, soliciting donations for the work of individual teachers. With him on his journey through Georgia was the famous Harriet Beecher Stowe, author of the best-selling anti-slavery novel *Uncle Tom's Cabin*, and her brother, Charles Beecher, who in 1871 was to become Florida's superintendent of public instruction. Two years after the trip that took her to St. Marys, Harriet was to buy 30 acres of land in Mandarin, Florida, and set about building a church and a school there for the support of local freedmen, in what would become her second home.

Happening upon Mary Richards and her school was not as accidental as Kennedy's report suggested. Harriet's brother, Henry Ward Beecher, had accompanied Mary at the Bridge Street church in New York when she had given her talk there, and the two had presumably kept in touch. He would have known where to find Mary, and led his sister and Reverend Kennedy to St. Marys to meet her.

Kennedy was quick to understand why Mary was the most suitable person to run the school in that area. "No white teacher would be tolerated there," he reported—if indeed anyone, other than Richards, would be willing "to go to such a desolate and isolated place." It was support for Mary's argument, in her first letters to the Freedmen's Bureau, that her involvement in St. Marys was badly needed. Kennedy noted how the mill chimneys, among the few structures left standing by the Union troops, stood guard over the charred ruins of the town. The legacy of Sherman's scorched earth policy was not only physical, but psychological. In the opinion of one freedman, the chimneys had not been demolished after the war in order to sustain the resentment of white Southerners—"to keep the anger of the people up." In this part of Georgia, memories of the trauma of the war were still fresh and raw for blacks and whites alike; and so was the hostility of white people towards newly liberated blacks.

Kennedy was fascinated by Mary Richards and her life story. She had, he wrote in his letter to *The American Freedman*, "a wonderful history." Mary had told him that her mother was "a white lady," and her father "a mixture of the Cuban-Spaniard and negro." If this account of her parentage is puzzling, it is also, we must suppose, inaccurate. A child of a white mother would have been legally a free person, even if of mixed race, and we know that Mary was born into slavery. Raised in a slave-holding and intensely racist society, she was acutely sensitive about her ethnic origins, and, as we have seen, boasted of what she considered her "advantages" of "Blood and Intelligence." It is possible that she did not want to tell these white upper-class visitors that she had been born a slave—although these three dedicated abolitionists were unlikely to have thought the worse of her for that. On the other hand, Kennedy could have got Mary's story wrong. The rest of his report stands on firmer ground:

> She was educated at Princeton, New Jersey, and went to Liberia as a teacher, where she remained about four years. On returning, she went to Richmond, and while appearing as a slave, was in the secret service of the U.S. She could write a romance from her experience in that employment.

Kennedy clearly enjoyed his visit to St. Marys. He and his friends stayed for tea with "this sister of ours," whose story "had brought tears into all our eyes." His main response to Richards' current situation, however, was not sentimental, but practical. She was evidently not receiving from her employers the help and encouragement she deserved. When her visitors arrived, she had been teaching in St. Marys for roughly three weeks, but so far, in spite of her urgent request for educational supplies, no one seemed in any rush to supply her with books. Impressed with Mary and her embryonic school, Kennedy decided that Miss Richards was "well worthy of support." He promised to send away for books for St. Marys as soon as he got back to New York. To emphasize the urgency, he put the request in his letter to *The American Freedman*:

> Miss Richards will sell what she can at the invoice prices, and return the money to the Association, and I am sure that what she gives away will be donated by the Executive Committee, for the colored people of St. Marys are very poor.... Don't wait for any meeting, but ship at once.

Charles Beecher, who, like Crammond Kennedy, was passionate about freedmen's education, promised to issue an appeal to his own Sunday school for funds to buy "a library" for Mary. Like Kennedy, he was impressed by her, calling her "quite a character." In the only known detailed description of her physical appearance, he described her as "a Juno, done in somber marble ... her features regular and expressive, her eyes exceedingly bright and sharp, her form and movements the perfection of grace."

Harriet Beecher Stowe wrote her own account of the visit to Mary Richards in her "Letter from Florida," published in *The Watchman* magazine:

> We visited a colored lady of good education, who is at present engaged in conducting the freemen's schools in this place. Miss R. Richards, was for some years a teacher in Liberia, under the care and patronage of Gov. Roberts. Returning to this country in the beginning of the war, she found herself in Richmond, where she remained, doing all she could for our cause in the secret service. With great courage, energy, and adroitness, she many times succeeded in conveying the most critical and important information to Gen. Grant. It was most interesting to hear some of her accounts.

Stowe reported briefly on Richards' work in St. Marys, and also on the desolation of a place where life had been so violently disrupted: "She went with us to walk along the grass-grown, silent streets of the village. We went into some deserted gardens...."[10]

It is hard to overemphasize Stowe's reputation in the nineteenth century. *Uncle Tom's Cabin*, published in book form in 1852, after being serialized in *The National Era* the previous year, sold millions of copies in the U.S. alone. In the South, it attracted violent hostility for its powerful denunciations of slavery. If today the book is regarded as sentimental and patronizing in its stereotypical portrayals of blacks, in its time it proved a powerful tool in raising awareness of the abominable cruelties of the slave system. *Uncle Tom's Cabin* was admired across the world by people as diverse as Leo Tolstoy, George Eliot, the British statesman Lord Palmerston, and the young Vladimir Lenin. It became a staple of popular culture, with theatrical adaptations and even minstrel shows based on the original text. Curiously, Mary Richards does not mention that Stowe and her brother came with Crammond Kennedy to see her. One feels Eberhart might have been more impressed by the visit of the famous novelist and her approval of Mary's endeavors, than by the other visitors. Nor does Mary mention that her distinguished guests were so interested in her exploits in wartime.

For all her adventurous life and her undoubted heroism, Mary Richards, in her letter of March 10, reveals a surprisingly unworldly side to her character. The letter has a confessional tone, and shows her to be quite sensitive to criticism.

> Mr. Eberhart I fear I like to receive approbation from others too well, any way I do feel like another woman since I received your letters and have seen some of my friends than I did when Dr Mitchell came from Savannah and told me what you had heard about me, but I must cease your time is too precious for me to write such long letters to you.

Whatever that negative report, and whoever was spreading it about, Mary had evidently felt crushed by it. Alone in St. Marys, feeling emotionally vulnerable, she reached out to Eberhart as to a friend. But he was an engineer and former military officer, schooled in stoicism and self-restraint. The tone of her letter—frank, almost childlike in its eagerness to do well and to prove herself in the eyes of others—was perhaps not the best way to establish credibility with a man like Eberhart. From here on, one suspects, he regarded Mary Richards very lightly. He probably was quite unaware of Mary's heroic service during the war. If he had known of it, would he have regarded her differently?

Vigilantes

The war does not appear to us to be ended, nor rebellion suppressed ... [Former slaves] are turned over to the tender mercies of their former oppressors, full of hatred and rebellion as ever, and burning for revenge on somebody.

—Philip Bell, African-American editor of the *San Francisco Elevator*, writing in July 1865

By April 7, 1867, Mary could feel proud of her school and her students. "I feel that I have worked pretty hard," she wrote to Eberhart. The school was "getting along very well," and in her description of the children's accomplishments, one senses not only her pride, but also her affection for them:

> Thirty little bright-eyed contrabands, that the first of this year did not know a letter, are now at the end of the National Primer, and I feel that they have learnt many verses and many little hymns that they never heard of before and they are well supplied with books.

In a hint towards the financial difficulties that would soon become acute, she added, "By the by, does the Government help pay for the books?"

Two months later, on June 1, she wrote again to Eberhart to tell him her school was attracting praise from the local community: "The citizens say, the children are improved more ways than one." She begged Eberhart to come and see for himself. "The new schools are sometimes more interesting than the older ones," she wrote, trying to encourage him.

Certainly, Eberhart could not fault Mary's dedication. Even a bout of illness would not keep her from her work. Laid up in her room for two weeks with the "fever and the neuralgia" (perhaps a return of chronic malaria or some other tropical fever contracted originally in Liberia) she had refused to let the sickness stop her teaching. When she was too weak to go to the classroom, or even to sit up, she'd had the students come to her room in her lodgings, and "taught them each one lesson." She still did not feel completely well, she wrote, in a letter dated April 7, "but I am much better." She was proud to say that she had not entirely closed the school even for a day.

Georgia during Reconstruction was an uncomfortable place to be black, and still more to be a black woman not native to the area and engaged in offering education to freed slaves. Even some blacks in Georgia proved resistant to the idea of education for freed people. In Macon, in a letter of May 27, 1867, a Freedmen's Bureau agent complained about the squabbling of black preachers who regarded local people's financial support for schools as competition for scarce funds they wanted for their own benefit. They "worked against the schools," he wrote, because they "wanted churches to fleece their flock" through taking up collections from the congregations.

White hostility, however, posed a far more serious threat. Impoverished whites resented the sight of their former "social inferiors"—people they had been taught all their lives to despise—being offered chances of self-improvement. (In fact, African Americans remained the most disadvantaged group in terms of education, since vastly more funds were expended on schooling for white children in Georgia. In addition to this, the white schools were funded by taxes that blacks were required to pay, even though they received no benefit in return.)

While Mary Richards was busy teaching at St. Marys during the summer of 1867, the threat from whites was growing. Everywhere across Georgia, starting and maintaining schools for blacks was becoming more difficult and dangerous. In May, at a place called Talbotton, white vigilantes threatened to break up a meeting held to found an educational association—a preliminary to involving the local community in setting up a school. "On my arrival here," wrote Freedmen's Bureau agent William White, "I was told by the colored people that threats had been made by the whites that our meeting should not be held." All the same, local people went ahead with the meeting. A gang of white men forced their way into the church where it was in progress. They interrupted the session with insults and swearing, "just as though they had been in a gambling saloon." With calculated menace, someone clicked the trigger of a pistol. They did not have to do more—the chilling message got through.

"They frightened the colored so," White reported, "that they were afraid to organize an association."

In the same month, over in Pine Hill, Washington County, another bureau agent observed ruefully that there could be a sizable school in the town, if only "the enemies of the colored man will let us meet in peace." Such was the threat, however, that the agent thought the local whites needed to be "taught a lesson." "I may have to call on the strong arm of the law for protection," he wrote to his superiors in the bureau.

A month later, William White, the same man who had reported the intimidation in Talbotton, described another community where the people were "very anxious" to have a school, but "very afraid." In yet another town, white people refused to allow African Americans to use the local black church for classes.

In her letter to Superintendent Eberhart dated April 7, 1867, Mary wrote of her concerns regarding white hostility in her own locality: "Mr. Eberhart I wish there was some law here or some protection. I know the Southerners pretty well, and their present appearance is not at all favorable." Richards had been, as she put it, "in the service so long as a detective" that "I still find myself scrutinizing them closely." Her concern was not so much with the typical "open braggadocio" of whites in the community—she was used to that. More disturbingly, she noted a "sinister expression about the eye," and among certain white people, "the quiet but bitterly expressed feeling, that I know portends evil.... These secret societies are doing something [or] at least trying to do something."

For Mary, the threat came closer to home when Dr. Augustus Mitchell, who had encouraged her to set up the school in St. Marys and assured her she would be safe there, received a death threat. This was in spite of Mitchell's wartime service as a surgeon with the Confederate military. He was now employed by the Freedmen's Bureau, and therefore probably regarded by some as a traitor to the Southern cause. His friendship with the likes of Mary Richards had also doubtless been noticed.[1]

Richards' comment about "secret societies" was turning out to be prescient. The newly formed Ku Klux Klan was on the rise in Georgia. By March 1868 there were Klan units all across the state. They created widespread terror, with random assaults on blacks, death threats, arson attacks on black schools, churches and other meeting places, and murders of Republican political leaders. Teachers, too, could find themselves targets of violence. People became frightened to support Republican politicians, or even to involve themselves with freedmen schools. (The federal government would crack down on vigilantism in the 1870s, only to see the Klan and its acts of terror resurface decades later, in the early 1900s.)

A letter from a bureau agent, dated only "September 12" but probably written in the late 1860s, gives a good indication of the scale of lawlessness. Having enclosed an official report on recent events in Georgia containing "a few facts" about the situation, the agent warned his superiors that the report gives "but a faint idea of the intimidation and outrage practiced upon freedmen and officials" across the state. To gain any redress through the courts was, he continued, "simply impossible," and he urged that "Some steps must be taken" whereby "troops can be sent to protect many of our agents" or "they will be driven from the field." The letter is blotted in places to the point of illegibility and the signature is undecipherable, but the message is starkly clear.

Between January 1 and November 15, 1868, agents of the Freedmen's Bureau in Georgia reported 336 cases of murder or assault with intent to kill against freedmen across the state.[2] Most notorious was the Camilla "riot" of September 1868, in the town of that name near Albany. It was a tragedy that kept the Freedmen's Bureau busy for months, gathering testimony from witnesses and survivors.

The so-called "riot," which in recent years has been more appropriately renamed the Camilla Massacre, began on September 19, 1868. An unprovoked armed attack on a Republican rally, attended mainly by black people keen to exercise their newly acquired political rights, left twelve people dead and many others injured. The attackers and their supporters carried on for days afterwards, hunting down survivors with dogs and terrorizing the black community in a bid to prevent them from voting in November's presidential election. (It was not until 1998, that the people of Camilla acknowledged the killings there for the first time and commemorated the victims.)

Mary Richards had left St. Marys by the time of the Camilla Massacre, but amid the growing power of racist white supremacy, new racial segregation laws, the hounding from office of black elected officials, and the gradual exclusion of black people from public life, it would not have surprised her. "I am not one of the Radical sort," she wrote in her letter of April 7, 1867, to Eberhart. Nor was she "one to get frightened at a shadow," but she was sure white racists in the St. Marys community were planning violence:

There is something on the carpet, you know, "with a little whisky in them, they dare do anything," and their apparent good feelings and acquiescence is only a vail [*sic*] to hide their true feelings.

Eberhart, she imagined, might think she was overreacting, and she wanted to assure him she was not. "Do not think I am frightened and laugh at my letter, any one that has spent 4 months in Richmond prison does not be so easily frightened."[3]

She probably *was* afraid, or at least apprehensive, and she had good reason to be. Her overriding concern, though, as her letter made clear, was more public-spirited. The bureau officials needed to take the vigilante threat more seriously, she told Eberhart: "I am not I hope meddling but I fear that there is more room for watchfulness than the Authorities believe."

In spite of the growing danger, Mary did not want to abandon her work at St. Marys, where she knew she was making a difference. Her teaching was effective, her students were learning well, and many in the community were impressed by her positive influence on the children. Yet the numbers attending her school kept dwindling, whether through the inability of local blacks to pay for schooling, or owing to intimidation from white racists. Whatever the cause, it was becoming evident to the Freedmen's Bureau that, without financial support in such a remote area, the school at St. Marys would prove unsustainable in the long run. The tone of Mary's letters grew desperate. On June 1, she begged Eberhart repeatedly to visit and see her project for himself:

I have been expecting you here ever since I received your letter, but the first of June has come, and I have not seen you yet. I wish you would come, I want to see you, and I want you to see the school before it gets any smaller. I hope you will be satisfied.

She hoped that if Eberhart was impressed by her work, he might find a way to keep the school going. "I have not neglected my school," she continued, "and I shall not as long as I hold the position of teacher but please come." Likewise, she felt that, in the face of white hostility, she would be able to rely on her students to keep her safe: "There are many of them that I believe would, were it necessary, protect the school as well as the teacher," she assured Eberhart.

Mary's pleas and assurances went unheard. At last, she received instructions from the Freedmen's Bureau to close her school. The main reason, it seemed, apart from her own poor health, lay in the inability of the local families to pay her salary. The bureau was not, apparently, prepared to make up the shortfall in her income. She ended the school year of 1867 with a heavy heart: "I closed the school today. Captain Royall of this Post was present, every one is sorry."

"I regret exceedingly," she wrote again to Eberhart, that "I could not have the compensation of seeing you in my school." How could she not feel disappointed and undervalued when the superintendent had not taken the trouble to come and witness for himself what she had achieved?

No doubt Eberhart was besieged by correspondence, with every other letter bringing a new set of problems to his attention and not enough hours in the day to complete the work. For Mary, though, her school project mattered to her in ways Eberhart could not possibly have understood. For a woman whose roles in life had so often been assigned to her by others, and who had been obliged to fend for herself in lonely independence, the school—her school—had put her at the heart of things and drawn an appreciative community around her. In that little world shaped by her pioneering efforts, people had turned to Mary Richards as a mentor and a friend. In her simple phrase "Every one is sorry," a world of meaning resides.

Mary's last letter to Eberhart, dated June 27, was full of a sense of weariness. Now her hopeful project had come to an end, she wanted only to receive the back pay due to her, and leave. She was bitterly disappointed that the superintendent had never come to appreciate her work. "I regret never having seen you," she wrote again. "I am tired, please let me hear from you soon … please write and let me know about the money, please pay me as soon as you can. I want to go home."

Then comes something unexpected. About a month before she had written to Eberhart that she had married a man named "Mr. Garvin." Who this man was, where he had come from, his race, his age, his occupation, are all unknown. Eberhart seems not to have believed that she was even married to him: "Well, I can tell you that I am," she wrote in response, sounding offended, "but my husband has gone to Havana." The reasons for Eberhart's skepticism are, again, unknown. But why should she claim to be married, if she was not? Why was Eberhart apparently so reluctant to believe her?

Mary had been in St. Marys since February and had presumably met Mr. Garvin in or around the town, but it seems that a man from such an impoverished black community—"not of the best type of freedmen," as Mary herself had said—would not, unless he was employed as a seaman, have had the money necessary to travel to Havana. Possibly Mr. Garvin was white, but interracial marriage was illegal in Georgia. Indeed, the legality of Mary's marriage to this man is questionable for other reasons, too. On paper, she was still married to Wilson Bowser. He might have died, but there is no evidence of that. About a month later, in a letter of June 27, she told Eberhart, "I am alone here, so I want to get away." Mr. Garvin had clearly not returned from Havana, if that was where he had gone.

Mary signed her letter to Eberhart, "Mary J. R. Garvin," adding a PS: "Please don't direct to Miss Richards again will you." If she had told others she was married, her concern is understandable. If anyone learned that Eberhart still addressed her as "Miss," it could have started tongues wagging. She had put her life on the line for the Union, and to free her fellow African Americans, and Eberhart could not even do her the courtesy of calling her by her married name.

Mary's relationship with Gilbert Eberhart had clearly soured, but by September 16, 1868, she was writing to his successor, the new superintendent of education, Edmund Asa Ware. Ware was not a military man like his predecessor, but a scholar, shortly to be appointed president of Atlanta University, and a licensed preacher with connections to the American Missionary Association. Mary must have hoped for greater sympathy from him than she'd received from Eberhart. She wrote to him from Savannah:

> Mr. Ware
> Sir I write to ask you to please give me a situation as teacher in Atlanta or near it my health is much better and I feel that I will be able to teach the term out. [The Doctor] advised me to write to you immediately as he says he thinks you will give me a situation, I was compelled to give up my school at St. Marys last term owing to bad health and the failure of the people to pay my board. I prefer living in Atlanta as my husband's Co. is stationed there, but if he should leave before the term is out I will bind myself to teach the term out. I am anxious to get a school though near Atlanta, I have been teaching some time at different places Norfolk and Richmond Va and also in middle Florida it was from middle Florida I came to St. Marys I had a commission last term under the A.M.S. I have it still and other papers ... Please favor me with an answer as soon as possible.

Here was another surprise: The husband to whom Mary referred in this letter was not Mr. Garvin. It seems that he was not coming back from the Caribbean. Her married name, as she signed it, was now "Mrs. John J. Denman."

Mary's new husband was, she claimed, a federal cavalryman, therefore almost certainly a white man, whose unit was based in Atlanta. Referring to her past teaching experience, she told Ware, "If you will see my husband he will tell you all about it." How long Mary had known this man Denman is unknown. Only three months before she had told Gilbert Eberhart that she was married to Mr. Garvin. The same questions of legality arise relating to bigamy and interracial marriage in Georgia.

She was clearly anxious to dispel any impression of unreliability, and assured Ware that her doctor thought her well enough to take up a new teaching post, and had encouraged her to apply. She promised to "bind herself" to work till the end of the school term, even if her husband was posted away from Georgia. It seems strange, however, that Mary would name this new husband as a witness to her past teaching experience. Was she invoking male authority here, to back her up? Or seeking to convince Ware that Denman really existed, and was not simply a convenient invention on her part to secure a post in Atlanta?

Whatever the facts of her situation, Ware's reply to Mary's request put an end to her hopes of employment with the Freedmen's Bureau anywhere near Atlanta. He wrote back to her on September 18, almost by return, saying that AMA was indeed the organization that supplied teachers to Atlanta, but unfortunately the list was "full for the present," and that what posts might have been available in that area were already taken. Moreover, the situation of the bureau itself, and the educational programs that depended on it, was now, he said, "quite unsettled." However, as if to avoid completely dashing Mary's hopes, he added that it was probable he would be both "able and glad" to employ her in the Savannah region "in the course of a month or two." He promised to add her name to his waiting list of applicants, and write again to her as soon as a vacancy came up.

This was hardly what Mary had wanted to hear, but she had to admit that Ware had offered her what little he could at the time.

A major reason for the "unsettled" state of affairs for the Freedmen's Bureau in Georgia was the accession to the U.S. presidency of a Southern Democrat, Andrew Johnson, after the murder of Abraham Lincoln.

Johnson had no reason to love the bureau. Its various activities were widely hated by his support base of white manual workers, small tradesmen, and farmers. A former slave owner, Johnson opposed the federal enactment of civil rights legislation awarding citizenship to blacks. He also battled, if unsuccessfully, to block legislation renewing funding for the bureau. In any case, the bureau's programs were always chronically underfunded, never coming anywhere near meeting the total need, or giving Southern blacks the economic empowerment that could have transformed their social and political situation. Even after 1869, under the Republican administration of President Ulysses S. Grant, support for the bureau remained half-hearted, and funding from Congress continued to be lacking. After 1870, when the right of African Americans to vote was formally ratified by the 15th Amendment to the U.S. Constitution, hostility and manipulation in the Southern states saw to it that black voters were prevented from using their vote. Would-be voters were blocked at voting booths by the implementation of a literacy test or an unaffordable tax, or by outright intimidation. For aspiring politicians wanting to uphold the rights of black people, there were few votes to be had anywhere. White

Southerners, meanwhile, were busily clawing back land ownership and control of the courts and local legislatures, while federal officials looked the other way. Officials of the Freedmen's Bureau found their efforts on the ground thwarted, and their own persons increasingly under threat. In such a climate, where white racists were steadily regaining the upper hand and black people were being frightened away from voting booths and schoolrooms, what hope was there for Mary Richards to find a new teaching post?

In a letter of July 25, 1868, to a Freemen's Bureau agent in Georgia, the head of the bureau in Washington, Colonel Caleb Sibley, announced the phased de facto withdrawal of all agents from the state. They would no longer enjoy even limited military protection. They might remain as "friends and advisers" to the freedmen, but "with no more authority than any other citizen." Many of their roles would be transferred to local justices of the peace. Although agents thus were given a choice to remain in a personal capacity, many had to leave Georgia altogether "for considerations of personal safety." The work of the educational department was able to carry on under the auspices of religious and charitable societies, although not without considerable personal risk to everyone involved.

By 1870, the U.S. federal government had ordered the withdrawal from Georgia of nearly all officers of the Freedmen's Bureau. Two years later, all bureau programs were ended for good. By then Mary had given up her quest for a teaching post near Atlanta, and was on her way out of the state, to begin a new life elsewhere.

Alone Again

I hope you will not lose sight of me.

What happened in Mary's life during the next two years remains largely a mystery. We know only one fact about this time—that her marriage to John Denman did not last.

Probably her relationships with both Garvin and Denman were based on informal contracts—"common law" verbal agreements. This assumption is borne out by the fact that John Denman, after he left the military in August 1869, married a woman named Margaret Fancher in Alabama, in March of the following year. When he died in 1929, Margaret inherited his pension. It is hard not to believe that Denman, and possibly Garvin before him, formed a union with Mary merely as a convenience—that for him she was a "war bride," to keep him company and satisfy his sexual needs until such time as he could go back home to his own people. (Sadly, this is a common enough story in wartime.)

Mary may genuinely have loved John Denman, but there could have been an aspect of convenience for her, too, in this partnership. Bearing a married name would have brought her greater respect when living on her own in an isolated community; and if she felt physically threatened, she had the protection—or at least the hope of protection—of a federal soldier. Whatever the case, Mary seems to have opted to consider herself still married to John Denman, even after he had left her for someone else. Eight months after he had remarried, she continued to call herself Mary Denman.

The next turn in the fortunes of Mary Richards, now Denman, only came to light in recent years when, in 2019, a letter turned up for sale at Cowan's Auction House. It was written in late 1870 to Elizabeth Van Lew, from her protégée, Mary Richards Denman, who was by then living at 30 Bedford Place, Brooklyn, New York.[1]

There is little doubt the letter is genuine. If Mary had been a national celebrity and a magnet for autograph collectors, there might have been an incentive for forgery, but her brief and limited period of postwar fame was now long past. In New York, she was simply one more unemployed black schoolteacher, struggling to make a living among people who knew nothing about her, and cared even less. The idiosyncratic handwriting in the letter—the quirky shape of the capital I's like crochet hooks, with the hook opening facing to the right—and the headlong style, with its cheerful disregard for punctuation and abrupt shifts of topic, are all familiar from Mary's earlier letters to the Freedmen's Bureau. In the letter, dated October 31, Mary wrote:

> My dear Miss Bet
> I suppose you are somewhat displeased with me. But I hope you will withdraw your displeasure when I give you my reasons for not accepting your kind offer but I was much better when I received your letter, and being in need of a dress and also owing some money, so I took the money for that purpose.

After the apology for not using Elizabeth's money as her patron had intended, the letter takes an unexpected turn. Elizabeth, it seems, had invited Mary to come back to stay with her. Mary, though, had declined the offer:

> ... if I could have a room to myself and been sure of saving enough to help support myself I should have come to Richmond. I am a woman now of thirty years of age and very quiet rather peculiar. I could not stay in the room with anyone else it would worry me to death. I then reconsidered the past, if I ever came to your house and you ever told me of what you had done for me I should wish myself anywhere else except there and during my stay there before ... I was often the source of trouble and you often reminded me of all your kindness to me, Now Miss Bet if I could do any thing to show you my gratitude I would do it, but that is impossible, therefore as long as I can get an existence for myself I must try.

Not for the first time in her eventful life, Mary found herself struggling to make her way in the world, far from the place of her birth. Like so many who would migrate to the great cities of the East Coast in the latter half of the nineteenth century, she was asserting her independence—hoping to build a new life for herself, far from her Southern birthplace. She explained how she proposed to do it:

> I have a sewing machine that I have to pay for monthly at the end of six months it will be mine. I don't get much work yet but I hope to get a great deal after a while. I think it would be unwomanly for me to become so dependent on anyone? … I must do as many others have done before.…

She had at least found temporary shelter in the city "staying with a family I knew in Princeton, and the girls were my school mates." She did not expect to be a seamstress for ever—she had career plans: "I expect to attend the teachers Normal school this winter and improve myself then the first vacancy that comes under the auspices of this board I will get it.…"

In 1870, Elizabeth Van Lew still held the post of Richmond's postmaster general, her reward from the administration of President Ulysses S. Grant for her wartime service to the Union. It was a lucrative position, in which she was proving an able and progressive administrator. Though later she would be driven from office by place-seeking opportunists envious of her success, and end her life in relative poverty, for now she was financially well placed to offer help to Mary.

From Elizabeth's viewpoint, Mary's returning to live with her in Richmond was an arrangement of mutual advantage. Now in her early fifties, she was almost as socially isolated as Mary, snubbed and insulted by hostile neighbors and former friends who regarded her as a traitor. Her only company at home was that of her servants. Elizabeth found herself, as she would later write, "as utterly alone in the city of my birth, as if I spoke a different language."[2] With so few people she could confide in, she had thought now of Mary—intelligent, forthright and outspoken, who had shared her experiences of wartime commitment and danger—as an ideal companion for her in old age.

From Mary's perspective, though, matters looked rather different. As she pointed out in her letter, she was now a mature woman, living her own life. She would come back to Richmond only if she could be sure of a room to herself, and financial independence.

Although she knew Elizabeth would be offended even by a polite rejection of her invitation, Mary's refusal was firm. Not, "If I had independent means I would come to Richmond"—but, "I should *have* come." With that use of the third conditional, she had closed the door on any possibility of negotiation.

As if to stress that her refusal was final, she added that she had become somewhat "peculiar." Her only evidence for this claim, however, was that sharing a room would "worry" her "to death." Hardly, one would have thought, much proof of eccentricity. Perhaps Mary simply meant that hers was a strong personality, one that made it hard for her to relate to or become very intimate with others. Given that her three marriages were so short-lived, it seems possible her husbands found her too forceful and feisty. Women in the nineteenth century were expected to be gentle and compliant. Mary may have been a woman some men—and some women too—found it difficult to deal with.

Mary's letter is shot through with ambiguity, full of shifts and turns—not least in her implicit resentment of her patron, which bubbles to the surface and becomes explicit with her next words: "I then reconsidered the past...." Mary could not forget how Elizabeth had harped on the subject of her own goodness—constantly reminding her of how kind she had been. Mary dreaded a revival of these recitations of benefits bestowed: "If I ever came to your house and you ever told me of what you had done for me I should wish myself anywhere else." (Had the two women actually had a falling out?)

But then an apologetic note creeps in again. Mary admitted she often gave Elizabeth "trouble" in the past that led Elizabeth to lecture her on her "kindness" to her protégée. What "trouble" was Mary referring to? We know about the problems in Liberia, when Elizabeth paid the fare home for the adolescent missionary; and the arrest in Richmond shortly after her return, when the Van Lew women might have blamed her for leaving the house without a pass, but all the same bailed her out of custody and brought her home safely. There may have been other incidents too; the strong-willed, assertive Mary could never have had an easy path through life in the racist South.

In the next line, however, she returns to asserting her independence. She would not be beholden to Elizabeth, since they could never have a relationship of equals. It was not chiefly a matter of money or social status, but of Mary's debt of gratitude to her patron, which she could never repay. And so she must stay on in New York and try to make a life for herself in the city. Presumably she could turn for help to her old friends from Princeton days, if anything really went wrong.

Her next remark, however, sounds an ominous note. If she did not succeed in her plan for teacher training, she wrote, "it will be through the failure of my health." We recall how illness had dragged at her, first in Liberia, then in Georgia, where it kept her from the classroom for days. Would she ever be well enough to make it through training college, let alone to work afterwards as a teacher?

Her letter ends with an appeal to Elizabeth: "I hope you will not loose [*sic*] sight of me...." From the brave assertions of maturity, and of hopes for economic independence, Mary reverts to the subject of her relationship with Elizabeth. As if fearing she might have gone too far in reproaching the older woman, and risked losing her friendship, she asks Elizabeth to stay in touch: "I cannot bear the thought that no one is interested in my weal or woe."

After a request for Elizabeth to send her official paperwork, and other personal items that she seems to have left at the Van Lew house—"some little things I do not want to lose"—there comes another surprising statement: "One great reason of my wishing to be alone, I have changed in all points from being no christian I have turned into a most bigoted catholic I mean Roman."

This sounds almost like an afterthought, to further justify her wish to be alone. But when she labels herself a "most bigoted" Catholic, is there more than a hint of aggressiveness in this assertion? Elizabeth, a devout Protestant, would hardly have been impressed to learn that her protégée had become a member of the Church of Rome. Mary may have been a woman of thirty, making her own way in the world, but is there not something here of a rebellious adolescent seeking to shock a parent, as she breaks free of the maternal apron strings?

From assertiveness, the letter closes with fondness: "God help you. Good night, my dear friend. Yours affectionately ..." Then, in another shift of tone—as if this intimacy might have seemed excessive, she ends with formality: "Yours affectionately—M. J. Denman."

Since the letter is signed with Denman's name, it seems Mary wanted to impress on Elizabeth that she considered herself still married.

It is a brave letter, with its claims to self-reliance, its plans for the future. All the same, underlying the assertiveness we may detect the loneliness. Mary was adrift again, with a need for emotional connection—for love. Brave, certainly, but also, in the last analysis, forlorn and full of uncertainty.

Uncertain for us, too, reading her letter more than 150 years later. After this last scrap of evidence of her presence in the world, Mary Richards Denman disappears from history.

Myth Makers

The spy who set fire to the Confederate White House.[1]

Given the many enigmas and unknowns in the life of Mary Richards, and the fascination of her story, it was inevitable that myths would come to be spun around the bare facts. Where hard information is so scarce, people have constantly been drawn to fill in the blanks in our knowledge with tales of their own, making up what they could not know. Sometimes the inaccurate inventions seem designed to explain a biographical gap. Where did Mary gain her education in the North? How did she end up working for Jefferson Davis? How did she somehow manage to lose not one, but three, different husbands?

It is not known what became of Mary Richards after she moved to New York: whether she lived on into old age or succumbed early to the ill health that had dogged her all through her twenties. We do not know if she remarried, had children, or found a way to carry on teaching. She might have gone back to Virginia and been buried in Richmond or some smaller town, or perhaps she stayed in New York for the rest of her life. And was she still alive when Elizabeth Van Lew died in 1900? It is only in recent years, one and a half centuries on, that renewed interest in sifting fact from fiction and more accurately documenting the life of this intriguing woman has begun in earnest.

It has long been common for narrators to invent what they do not know about Mary Richards and present it as fact. This tradition began with William Beymer's 1911 article in *Harper's Monthly*, where we have the unlikely scenario of Elizabeth Van Lew, a known opponent of the Confederacy, personally contacting Varina Davis to recommend Mary as a servant to the Davis family.

The errors and confusions continue with Mary's name. She is often referred to as Mary Bowser, even though she herself had gone back to using her maiden name by the end of the Civil War, and had two more married names thereafter. She was never called "Ellen Bond" either, although this claim can be found repeated all over the more gossipy reaches of the internet; for instance in the podcast *Good Witches, Bad Bitches*: "In order to get access to top-secret information, Bowser became 'Ellen Bond,' a slow-thinking, but able, servant."[2]

That Mary was educated in Philadelphia by Quakers once seemed plausible, given that her patron Elizabeth Van Lew had received her own education in the city and retained many social connections in Pennsylvania. However, when Crammond Kennedy told of his visit to Mary in Georgia, he mentioned her schooling in Princeton, New Jersey. Then, in 2019, when Mary's letter of 1870 came to light, in which she mentioned women she knew as her schoolmates in Princeton, the Philadelphia education theory was conclusively shown to be speculation born of the frustrating gaps in our knowledge of someone we long to know better.

It is disappointing to find that the photograph once regularly reproduced as belonging to this hero of the Civil War has turned out to be of a different Mary Bowser altogether. The face in this portrait looks fairly young—of a woman in her thirties, possibly. But in 1900, when the photo was taken, Mary would have been sixty. Moreover, when we last hear of *our* Mary (in 1870), she was not calling herself Mrs. Bowser, but Mrs. Denman.

Some tales about Mary Richards are clearly intended to make her story more exciting—as if the known facts were not compelling enough in themselves. For instance, the legend that Mary set fire to the White House of the Confederacy before she fled from there. We know that there was a fire in the house, which was quickly put out, but it is most unlikely that the discreet, cautious Mary would have started it and risked breaking her cover, putting herself and her mission in danger. The story that when the war ended and the Davis family fled, Mary was smuggled out of Richmond in a cart is also an invention (though she may have left in a cart—we simply do not know).

There are many other baseless cloak-and-dagger stories about how Mary accomplished her mission in the Davis household. Karen Abbott, author of *Liar, Temptress, Soldier, Spy: Four Women Undercover in the Civil War*, tells of how Mary allegedly sewed coded messages into the hems and seams of Varina Davis's dresses. The clothes were then supposedly delivered to a fellow agent, a seamstress in Richmond, who extracted and decoded the information. Although given out as history, the tale of messages hidden in clothing does not belong to Mary, but to a seamstress who worked for Eliza Van Lew's neighbors, the Carringtons.

This woman, like Elizabeth and Mary, was active in the Richmond underground.[3]

It is often tempting to make up what one wishes to be true. A case in point is the legend of the Mary Bowser journal. As late as the 1960s, the Bowser family living in Richmond—descendants of Mary's husband Wilson Bowser—recalled how their ancestors had avoided speaking about Mary "because she was a spy." Even after the Civil War, and although the marriage to Wilson had been so short-lived, apparently they still feared possible retribution from racists. One descendant, Mrs. McEva Bowser, claimed to have come across a diary kept by Mary that presumably had been handed down through the family. Mrs. Bowser was cleaning the room of her recently deceased mother-in-law when, she said, "I ran across a diary."

> But I never had a diary and I didn't even realize what it was.... And I did keep coming across references to Mr. Davis. And the only Davis I could think of was the contractor who had been doing some work at the house. And the first time I came across it I threw it aside and said I would read it again. Then I started to talk to my husband about it but I felt it would depress him. So the next time I came across it I just pitched it in the trash can.[4]

Unfortunately, as Mrs. Bowser disposed of the diary without reading it, we shall never discover the author's true identity. Davis is, though, a fairly common name. Would Mary really have risked keeping a journal about her experiences during the war—even after the war had ended? Only if she had been very careful about what she had written in it. It may be recalled how cautious she was in her accounts of her wartime activities when speaking publicly to the audiences in New York. We know that Elizabeth Van Lew destroyed most of her own diary entries and other wartime personal records almost immediately after writing them. We also might wonder why Mary's diary would have been left with a member of the Bowser family, when by 1867, and possibly much earlier, she had separated from those in-laws for good.

Mary Richards' own narratives about herself at times add to the confusion: her use of pseudonyms; her claim to be of Hispanic descent; her dramatic, and unfounded, tale of having been sold into slavery as an adult; and the smokescreen of inventions she threw across her wartime doings. Some of her stories of the war years in her public talks sound far-fetched, but could equally be true. She apparently married three times—but when last heard from she was without a husband, living miles from her Southern birthplace, confronting an unknown future. No wonder the search for definite information about the historical Mary is both so intriguing and so tantalizing.

Not surprisingly, given the myths and the mysteries, but above all, the inspiring example of her cleverness and courage, the Mary Richards legend has proved irresistible to writers of fiction, adding further layers of confusion to the bare facts of Mary's biography. Imaginative inventions by novelists and movie makers, taken at face value, are all too easily mistaken for established facts.

At least three novels, two films, and a stage play have been based on elements of the Mary Richards story. These works are discussed below, in roughly chronological order.

A Special Friendship

TV Movie, 1987—CBS network, March 31, 1987
Directed by Fielder Cook. Script by Kenneth Cavander
With Akosua Busia as Mary Bowser and Tracy Pollan as Elizabeth Van Lew

As the title suggests, the focus of Cook's film, which takes considerable liberties with known biographical facts, is the relationship between Mary Richards and Elizabeth Van Lew. Young Mary in the film is not represented as having been born in the Van Lew household, but bought by Elizabeth's father, John, along with Mary's parents, in Richmond's slave market. Elizabeth, portrayed here as a child only a few years older than Mary, is shown to be delighted that the slave family have not been separated. (In a further departure from history, it is John Van Lew who leaves instructions in his will to free the family slaves—not his widow, who as we know disobeyed his explicit instructions to retain the human property in bondage.) Elizabeth and Mary soon form a close friendship, transcending barriers of race and social rank. It is young Elizabeth who discovers Mary's intelligence, who teaches her in secret, and who insists—against her mother's opposition—on having Mary sent to the North to receive further education.

By the time the Civil War breaks out, Elizabeth is a marriageable young Southern belle—not a mature woman in her early forties as the historical Elizabeth Van Lew was by then, but a lovely blonde heroine in the classic Hollywood mold.

It is not long before a character clearly based on Thomas McNiven—in the film he is known only by his codename "Quaker"—approaches the idealistic but naive young Elizabeth, to sound her out about helping him in resisting the Confederacy. Meanwhile, Mary Richards is installed as a supposed slave in the Davis household, and her spying career begins. This part of the narrative is well handled, with a convincing script. Akosua Busia gives a most credible performance as the new servant, who has to appear both illiterate and somewhat witless. Surprised in the act of poring over documents spread out on a table, Cavander's character gets away with it by pretending to be fascinated by the curious shapes of the letters she supposedly cannot read.

Less convincing, from a narrative point of view, are the scenes in which Mary repeatedly travels up and down to a Union encampment, carrying messages to the military commanders. (How would she find time off from drudging for the Davis family, and not be missed from the household?)

In this story, Mary is deeply in love with a young man from a middle-class black Northern family. They hope to make a life together, but he is killed on the battlefield while fighting for the Union. Elizabeth, meanwhile, is engaged to the son of Richmond's governor, General Winder. But she grows ever more estranged from him as she and the young man find themselves on opposite sides in the conflict: She, rescuing escaped prisoners and gathering intelligence for the Union; and he, working to root out Union spies. In the end, Elizabeth is arrested and held for questioning—something that never happened to the historical Elizabeth. Improbably, it is her fiancé who is assigned to conduct her interrogation. Brought face to face with the imprisoned "Quaker," who has been tortured, Elizabeth finally rejects her fiancé and the brutality he represents.

Elizabeth has been lured into a trap with disinformation, and now is accused of betraying the Confederacy. It is her friend Mary who exposes the falsehood, and springs her friend from prison. Mary then travels up to the Union lines to find the Union commander and correct the misleading intelligence, before the troops can be lured into an ambush. While in the army camp, she learns that her lover has been killed in battle.

Grief-stricken, Mary returns to Richmond, to a grateful reunion with Elizabeth, whom she embraces as her friend is let out of prison. They go back to the Van Lews' house to find a hostile crowd gathered around the entrance. They threaten the women and insult them. Mary climbs on a step and makes a speech. The jeering crowd fall silent as she tells them she has lost her man, a Union soldier, at the battle of Fredericksburg. She is sure many of them have also lost loved ones in "this damnable war." "Well," she tells the crowd, "this war's gonna be over soon, so what you want to keep up the hating for?" They are all going to have to learn to find a way to live together, she says, "so let's start learnin'... right now." Given the setting—besieged Richmond, where the Confederacy is on its knees—the history of slavery in the South, and the lowly status of a black female in that world, it seems most improbable that Mary's eloquent speech would cut much ice with hostile Confederates. Fortunately, she does not hang around to study their reaction, and nor do we, the audience. The women go up the entrance steps and into the house, the subdued crowd slowly disperses, and the film ends.

The Secrets of Mary Bowser
Lois Leveen. London: Hodder & Stoughton, 2012

The conventions of romantic fiction weigh heavily on *The Secrets of Mary Bowser,* and at times threaten to capsize it into melodrama. The novel's great strength, it must be said, is Leveen's meticulously researched accounts of how life was lived in America in the nineteenth century. Her detailed knowledge of customs and material data—of the housing conditions of people of all classes from slaves to the gentry, her informed descriptions of medical practices, of foods and their preparation, of the kind of vehicles different people drove in different situations, and of class interactions and social expectations, make for richly textured evocations of the world of nineteenth-century America, North and South. Leveen gives us a social world we can believe in—a solidly detailed background, against which her story unfolds.

Leveen is also the one author whose fiction gives really detailed attention to imagining Mary's schooling. She can hardly be faulted for setting that experience in Philadelphia rather than Princeton, New Jersey, or for inventing an elite academy with a Quaker teacher, where Latin is taught, and the students are drawn from the cream of black Philadelphia society. When Richards' letter to Elizabeth Van Lew came to light, seven years after publication of *The Secrets of Mary Bowser*, it became possible to reconstruct a very different educational experience for Mary.

It is when Leveen's story encounters the traditions of popular fiction that the novel opens itself to criticism. It is not enough, apparently, for Leveen's Mary to have been discreetly spying in the Jefferson Davis household. She has to be involved from her schooldays in aiding the escape of slaves along the Underground Railroad, and—as in *A Special Friendship*—personally involved in dangerous missions (as if her role in the Davis household was not already dangerous enough), carrying coded messages up to the Union lines. When she and her companions are threatened by a violent white man, she knocks the attacker unconscious—then, overtaken by a bout of rage, shoots the man and stamps on his head. (At least this incident, for which Leveen's character later feels intense guilt, is justified by an earlier debate in the novel, where supporters of non-violent abolitionist campaigns are challenged by believers in the use of force.) But the story of Mary's experiences in the Davis household, and in the surroundings of Richmond, surely would have been dramatic enough, without any such sensational embellishment.

Characterization in *The Secrets of Mary Bowser* sometimes deviates from what we know of historical characters. Unlike in *A Special Friendship*, Leveen's Elizabeth Van Lew is at least assigned an age that sets her in the relationship to Mary of employer, patron, and parent figure, in agreement with biographical fact. It is difficult, though, to square Leveen's fictional representation of Elizabeth with what we know of her as the discreet, savvy administrator of a highly successful network of spies, and then a capable and innovative postmaster general. Leveen's Van Lew, by contrast, is shown as foolish, garrulous, vain, and self-regarding—a woman with more idealism than common sense. One cannot imagine anyone trusting this character to go out and buy a pound of butter, let alone to coordinate a spy ring in wartime.

To keep her central character firmly in the foreground, Leveen attributes many of Van Lew's historically recorded successes in intelligence gathering, to Mary. At one point, the main protagonist is even credited with exerting a major influence on the course of the war, when she deliberately withholds a crucial piece of military information that could have shortened the conflict and brought a decisive Union victory. She chooses not to send it because she wants to ensure that the war continues until Lincoln has made up his mind to free the slaves.

As in other fictional versions of Mary Richards' story, Leveen assigns her character known parents: a mother, freed from slavery by the Van Lews, who lives with her daughter in the Van Lew household; and an enslaved father, owned by a master who refuses to free him even for an offer of payment. Mary is also given an enduring, close relationship with Wilson Bowser. In a further clear departure from actual biography, where the historical Mary had probably separated from Bowser well before the war's end (and had returned to using her maiden name), Leveen's fictional marriage is depicted as still going strong after the war, and likely to last. (The story is not pursued to Mary's move to Georgia and her two later relationships, so that the illusion of long-term monogamy is sustained.)

Assigning Mary solid family ties she almost certainly did not have was, Leveen explained in a later commentary on her novel, deliberate on the author's part:

> In *The Secrets of Mary Bowser*, I gave Mary what I wish she truly had: doting parents, a devoted husband who is fully supportive of her intelligence work, and a savvy and sensitive best friend with whom she navigates adolescence and early adulthood. In real life, she may never

have known any of those things. Enslaved people persistently struggled to create the best and most loving lives they could. But even under what whites touted as the "kindest" manifestations of slavery, black families were perilously vulnerable, as Mary's own life shows. Though the Van Lews singled her out from childhood for special treatment by bringing her to their own church to be baptized and sending her north to be educated, their benevolence did not include preserving her connections to her own family. That is a devastating price to pay for freedom.

In Leveen's view, Mary's letter to Elizabeth of 1870 "confirms that the repercussions of this loss continued to echo for Mary long after the war, leaving her without any semblance of family and community on whom she could consistently rely." This, for Leveen, is both a personal tragedy, and that of an entire society: "Her espionage contributed to the abolition of slavery in this country, yet the legacy of slavery still burdened her. And in myriad ways, it still burdens all of us."[5]

And yet—as Leveen implicitly recognizes—Mary Richards' solitude in life, the lonely survivor's independence that solitude bred in her and the self-reliance she developed, were crucial to the person she became, and probably to her ability to carry out her mission in wartime. She was used to coping alone. She possessed the "cool and lonely courage" a spymaster once spoke of in the context of a different group of female agents, and a different war.[6]

Whatever one may think of Leveen's fictional portrayal of individual historical characters in *The Secrets of Mary Bowser*, or the far-fetched incidents in which she embroils her character, she must be given her due for her thorough and ground-breaking research—and for the atmosphere of the period she evokes through an accumulation of thoughtful detail.

Lady Patriot
Stage play by Ted Lange
First performed September 7, 2012, at the Hudson Theatre, Los Angeles
Directed by Ted Lange, with Chrystee Pharris as Mary Bowser and Connie Ventress as Elizabeth Van Lew
Bloomington, Indiana: Trafford Publishing, 2013

> I feel compelled to tell the story less known ... the history of those in the shadow of the victor.

Ted Lange, perhaps best known for his TV acting roles, has built a second reputation as the author of over twenty-four plays. He works mainly with subjects drawn from black history—stories that particularly resonate with him as an African American exploring his heritage. As he told a journalist in 2017, he writes to "expand" Americans' existing historical knowledge, affording wider perspectives on the national story. In particular, he seeks to bring forgotten, heroic, black individuals into the limelight. Mary Richards is a case in point:

> If you read history books about that era, Mary Bowser is either not in the book, or she's just a footnote. So [in *Lady Patriot*] I brought her to the forefront, and told it from her point of view.[7]

Lady Patriot is the third play in Lange's historical trilogy about seminal events in early American history. The first tells the story of a slave named William Lee, who was valet to George Washington (*George Washington's Boy*, 2007). The second, *The Journals of Osborne P. Anderson*, is the narrative of the only black person to survive the abortive raid of John Brown at Harper's Ferry. *Lady Patriot,* the last in the series, has proved the most popular work of the three. It has been widely performed in repertory across the United States, and has been translated into several European languages.[8]

Lange researched intensively to understand the figures of the three women at the center of his drama—Elizabeth Van Lew, Varina Davis, and Mary Richards Bowser. He read biographies, interviewed historians, and visited the former White House of the Confederacy (now renamed the American Civil War Museum, Richmond) to bring that setting to life in his drama. The première of *Lady Patriot* was directed by Lange himself, who also took the part of Jefferson Davis's elderly slave, Robert Brown.

Lady Patriot is mercifully free of melodrama, and there are moments of wit and humor. Personal tragedy enters the play—all the more movingly for being understated—in a chilling scene where Lange's Jefferson Davis coolly explains to the old slave Robert Brown the Davis family's business rationale for selling off Brown's beloved wife to an unknown fate. She had become unable to "breed," Davis tells the old man, and it was uneconomic to keep her: "she lost her value." Nothing, though, is allowed to enter this play of Elizabeth Van Lew's agonized and haunted reflections on slavery, as they appear in her Civil War diary. Nor do we hear much of Varina's doubts about the wisdom of secession, or about her husband's fitness for the role of Confederate president. It is left to the fictional character of a visiting Northern journalist to evoke the wasteful, tragic carnage of the war.

When we first encounter Lange's Mary, she is being lectured by Elizabeth: "No, no, no, no Mary! Don't be stupid.... Mess with me, I'll make you feel lower than a toad in a dry well." Mary, meanwhile, says little to Van Lew in return, except for a repeated, submissive, "Yes, 'em." Only after Robert Brown, who has come to escort Mary to the Davises' house, has gone out for a moment, do we realize the two women have been acting a part for his benefit. Once they are alone, Elizabeth hugs Mary, and "in a softer tone … almost a whisper," wishes her luck in her mission.

Like others before him, in dealing with the Mary Richards/Mary Richards Bowser story, Lange takes liberties with history. In particular, he portrays a friendship between Van Lew and Varina Davis that almost certainly never existed in life; but it affords a means of contrasting the two women's personalities. Varina is depicted as ladylike, fastidious, a doting mother and wife, ever anxious about her impending childbirth, and later in the play, afraid for the fate of her husband as the defeat of the Confederacy draws near. She is shown as living in the shadow of Davis's obsession with his deceased first wife, and escaping from her troubles by resorting to frequent swigs of absinthe. Lange's Van Lew is practical, generous, down-to-earth, and given to earthy expressions: "I'm gonna stop by next week to make sure nobody pissed in the punch." Regarded by other characters as more than a little off her head, she is shown to be, in reality, clever and contriving, with her eccentric mannerisms a disguise for her skillful work as a spy. Lange humanizes her character by depicting her in a flirtation with the visiting Northern journalist—a character based on the nineteenth-century photojournalist and war reporter John Slidell. She feeds him secret information for export to the North, but also does her best to lure him into bed with her.

Another great strength of the play is the relationship between Mary, a young idealist passionately committed to the cause of black freedom, and the old slave Robert Brown, who has learned to adapt himself to his hopeless situation in life by carefully studying his master's wishes. Through observing the behavior of white people, he has become an astute practical psychologist: "Oh, I've seen 'em try to hide a secret, but I been around long enough to recognize a lie or see de truth … sitting right dere in dey eye." Out of everyone in the Davis household, only Robert sees through Mary's pretense of illiteracy. While she has to conceal from him her real motive for reading Davis's papers, she offers to teach the old slave to read and write. Near the play's close, as she is caught trying to set fire to the house (*Lady Patriot* accepts as fact this apocryphal detail of the "Mary Bowser" legend), her helpfulness to him is rewarded: She is able to persuade Robert to let her escape, and convinces him to join her.

An Extraordinary Union and *A Hope Divided*
Alyssa Cole. New York: Kensington Books, 2017

The first two novels in Alyssa Cole's much-praised and widely reviewed trilogy of historical romances set during the American Civil War, draw largely upon the biography of Mary Richards—her experience of growing up in the home of her abolitionist patron, and her career as a wartime spy. Cole weaves these themes into narratives about two different women, in two different settings. (The third novel in the series, *An Unconditional Freedom*, has no connection to Mary Richards, dealing as it does with the relationship between a man recently freed from slavery, and the mixed-race daughter of a Cuban slave-owner.)

An Extraordinary Union, the first volume in the trilogy, follows the Mary Richards story most closely, dealing with the adventures of a young black woman who goes underground posing as a slave, to gather intelligence in a wealthy Confederate household. In the second, *A Hope Divided*, we meet Marlie, a healer and partly self-taught herbalist, who has been raised in the home of an abolitionist. A free woman since the death of her female benefactor's father, Marlie is treated as "a member of the family," although never quite as an equal. In the Civil War, she works to help escaped Union prisoners make their way to the North and safety.

In her two composite fictional portraits, Cole gives us credible and attractive images of bold, intelligent, independent women. Their common legendary ancestor is easily recognizable as Mary Richards, with whom, through her own family history, Cole evidently feels a kinship. Herself of African-American descent, Cole dedicates *An Extraordinary Union* to "Isabell, the last enslaved person and the first emancipated person in my family's history."

A familiar pattern in Cole's "Loyal League" trilogy—so named for the fictitious spy ring to which many of the main characters belong—is that of a man and a woman actively committed to the Union cause, who find themselves working on the same patch, or otherwise thrown together by circumstance. After initial misunderstandings—and, at times, outright suspicion and hostility—the pair come to accept and respect one another. Yielding at last to the powerful erotic attraction that has been there between them all along, they give way to passionate sex and declarations of undying love. Both *An Extraordinary Union* and *A Hope Divided* end in a proposal of marriage.

In *An Extraordinary Union*, Cole's character Ellen—"Elle"—is a volunteer agent in the Loyal League. Like Mary Richards, she has recently returned from Liberia. In the fictional Ellen's case, we are told she went to Africa to make a new life for herself, only to feel herself an alien in the unfamiliar surroundings. Elle's superiors in the league regard her with skepticism, doubtful of her ability to function underground as a spy. She is determined to prove them wrong. In a reference to a part of the Mary Richards legend, one of her great assets is her phenomenal memory. Unlike Mary, however, Elle is the child of free parents. In Northern-born Elle's childhood, her mental gifts led to her being publicly exhibited as a prodigy in abolitionist circles.

Elle's chance to prove herself as an undercover agent comes when she is assigned to pose as a slave in the home of a wealthy Confederate senator, who regularly entertains guests with military connections. Like the original Mary Richards, Elle in the novel pretends to be illiterate. Cole also has her pretend to be mute—a situation that makes for extra plot complications whenever some emergency forces her to come out of character and speak.

Shortly after taking up her new role posing as a slave in the senator's house, Elle finds herself reluctantly working with a fellow agent. Malcolm McCall is a detective from the newly formed Pinkerton agency, which has sent him to Richmond to liaise with the agent from the Loyal League.

In a nod to Mary Richards' links to the Scottish spy Thomas McNiven, Malcolm is a Scot. Like the historical McNiven, McCall's family have emigrated from Scotland to America to escape from oppression by the English. At first, Elle resents McCall's conceited manner, while all the same finding him irresistibly attractive. Shared secrets, nights of clandestine love-making, and hair-raising life-or-death situations in which the two risk their lives for one another, make for a firm bond based not solely on lust, but on mutual trust, respect, affection, and loyalty. After Malcolm is imprisoned in the senator's house, accused of treason, Elle sets out to rescue him. In an allusion to the apocryphal story of Mary Richards' arson attempt on the White House of the Confederacy, Elle creates a fire-raising diversion to give herself time to reach the cellar where her lover is held.

The novel has a subplot in which Ellen and Malcolm save Elle's childhood sweetheart who has been kidnapped from the North and sold into slavery, arranging to buy his freedom. Elle's main achievement, though, is to discover a Confederate plan to build a new "ironclad" warship that is to be used in breaking the Union blockade around Southern ports. (As a matter of historical fact, this was an actual development in the war, though it was not, as far as we know, a piece of intelligence gathered by the historical Mary Richards.) To get the information to the Union forces before the vessel can be deployed in action, Elle escapes from Richmond with Malcolm, determined to hijack the warship and deliver it safely to the federal navy.

Although she adopts enough elements from Richards' biography to make the influences on her characters recognizable, Cole wisely does not try for any one-to-one correspondence between her fictional heroines and the historical Mary Richards. In *A Hope Divided*, the allusions go only as far as the details of the main character's family background. Marlie is the child of a white master and his enslaved mistress. Freed by the family and treated much as one of their own, she is encouraged to take part in work for the Loyal League at the outbreak of the Civil War. Beyond these points, any parallel with the biography of Mary Richards ceases. The fictional narrative now takes a quite different course, with Marlie on the run from being sold into prostitution. She journeys through the wilderness in search of safety in company with Ewan, an escaped prisoner of war who becomes her lover.

Working with a narrative that constantly alludes to biographical and legendary precedents, while evolving a wholly new story, is an effective strategy. It lends Cole's fiction the resonance of historical allusion, while at the same time giving her the freedom to take her romance in any direction she pleases.

Ellen Bond, Secret Agent
Movie trailer. Written in Stone Productions, 2018
Director and scriptwriter, Michael Paul Stone
With Enisha Brewster as Ellen Bond and Gloria O'Brien as Elizabeth Van Lew

With a down-to-earth portrayal of a middle-aged Elizabeth Van Lew, this trailer for a low-budget, crowdfunded film at first hews more closely to the historical narrative of Mary Richards' wartime exploits in the Davis household than the 1987 TV drama, *A Special Friendship*. A sparky Enisha Brewster is compelling in the role of "Ellen Bond," while she acts the part of a slow-witted, illiterate slave in the White House of the Confederacy. She is then energetically boyish, in pants and a rakish hat, as she travels in disguise to carry messages through the Virginia woods to the Union lines.

Inevitably, perhaps, as in most fictional adaptations of the Mary Richards story, the plot veers off into melodrama with an armed confrontation with Confederate soldiers, in which Ellen is injured.

Admittedly, we only have the trailer; but the film does not appear remarkable for the subtlety of its dialogue: "Mr. President, we have a spy in the Confederate White House—code name, Ellen Bond." As if one African-American heroine working undercover were not enough, a better-known secret agent makes a cameo appearance: "I'm so happy to finally meet you, Mrs. Tubman." "Call me Harriet."

What the film might lack in nuance, however, it seems more than likely to make up in drama—in powerful acting and gripping action scenes taking place in the woods at night.

Particular dramatic aspects of Mary Richards' war work have proved irresistible to novelists and scriptwriters. Mary's alleged phenomenal memory; her visits to the prisons, delivering humanitarian aid, but also picking up coded messages; her stint in the White House of the Confederacy posing as an illiterate slave with the constant threat of exposure; her quick-wittedness to avoid discovery every time capture threatened: All these elements have repeatedly found their way into fiction. But most authors of fiction cannot resist embellishing the story by the invention of sensational, often violent, imaginary incidents.

The heroines modeled on the exploits of Mary Richards are not only improbably mobile, given the crucial importance of her role in the Davis household (what vital intelligence might they miss out on, if they spent their time hurrying through the night to deliver messages?). They are depicted carrying out dramatic, improbable rescues of a friend or lover from Confederate clutches (a motif common to *A Special Friendship,* and to both Cole's novels). In *A Special Friendship*, as previously noted, Mary saves Elizabeth Van Lew from captivity. In *A Hope Divided*, Marlie rescues her lover Ewan from torture at the hands of the villainous Confederate officer Cahill, much as Ellen saved her Malcolm in the earlier novel. These fictional characters handle weapons. Sometimes they kill people—but always in self-defense.

It is interesting to consider what these fictional versions of Richards' eventful history—or the three decades that we know of it—leave out. Most focus almost exclusively on Mary Richards' experiences undercover during the Civil War; with the exception of Lois Leveen and Alyssa Cole in *An Extraordinary Union,* they give scant attention to her prewar schooling in the North or to her doings in what we know of her postwar years. Two elements in particular are invariably omitted from the stories based on Richards' life: her time as a teenage missionary in Liberia, and her experience afterwards, of founding a school for freed people in Georgia. Both these episodes must have affected her deeply—her four years in Liberia, if nothing else, probably left their mark in the form of chronic ill health. For Alyssa Cole's Ellen, Liberia is mentioned only as the place where her character felt herself to be an alien. In the other narratives, Liberia is not mentioned at all.

The pride Mary Richards felt in her Georgia school and in the progress of her pupils evidently motivated her to go on wanting to teach, and later, after her move to New York, to train to be better at it. But again, these episodes, however crucial in the life of the historical

Mary, have no place in narratives exclusively focused on romance and derring-do.

Almost none of the fictional works address the ambiguity, and Richards' own ambivalence, about her parentage. According to Crammond Kennedy, Mary said her father was Hispanic. At other times she said she never knew who her parents were. Those reimagining her story in fictional terms either leave the question of parentage aside or, more commonly, seem to feel compelled to assign their heroine a mother and father. Mary, or her fictional counterpart, is regularly portrayed as an only child of parents who, in the absence of siblings, pour all their affection on her. In *The Secrets of Mary Bowser* and *A Special Friendship*, Mary's parents are slaves, or former slaves, living in Richmond. In both the novel and the film, the mothers are presented as strict but caring; concerned that their daughter will grow up in a loving atmosphere, but anxious for her future in a white-dominated world where at any moment the masters can turn nasty and bring down the whip. Cole's *An Extraordinary Union* likewise assigns parents to her character Ellen, but makes her a child of free AfricanAmericans living in the North. (They will not, we are told, be best pleased when they learn their daughter is getting married to a white man.)

Only Cole's *A Hope Divided* has a black heroine, the daughter of an enslaved mother, who lives in a white abolitionist household in ignorance of her family origins. Marlie constantly questions her relationship to Sarah, the benefactor who will never call her "sister," until she learns what the historical Mary Richards probably never discovered—the truth about her parentage. (Cole has Marlie discover that Sarah's brother is her father—a secret that Sarah had long known, but had been keeping from her.)

It seems odd that novelists dealing with the painful and sensitive issues of family relations in slavery steer away from this central, tragic fact of so many slave lives—that children often had no idea who their parents were, and that parents whose children were sold away from them, could not know where their child was, or what had become of them. Mary Richards' own experience of unknowing and of being alone in the world except for her ambivalent relationship to Elizabeth Van Lew, is crucial to our understanding of the adult she became. The conventions of the nuclear family, though, even in imagining a character born into slavery, are, it seems, compelling.

Of all the writers of fiction based on the Mary Richards story, Cole comes closest to engaging with the predicament of a former slave living in a white family where she is as much a servant as a family member, and can never quite feel she belongs. It was a conflict that, we know, at times deeply troubled the historical Mary. In romantic fiction, however, such uneasy self-consciousness would lead to unwanted introspection. It would sit uncomfortably with fictional characters whose main role is to perform as relatively uncomplicated heroines in scenes of love and action. Too much interiority would get in the way.

Most of the fictional treatments based on Richards' life assign the heroine not only parents, but a husband or a lover in a lasting relationship. The question of why Mary Richards' marriage to Wilson Bowser had ended by the time the war was over is never addressed in fictional form—let alone her two equally short-lived marriages after that. Instead, there is deference to the notion of lifelong romantic love. Mary, or her avatars, must have a fulfilling heterosexual relationship—even if, as in *A Special Friendship*, the relationship is shown to end in tragedy.

In most of the fictional adaptations where Elizabeth Van Lew might be expected to feature, Van Lew's roles as spymaster, as Mary's employer, or as surrogate parent, are considerably downplayed. Often, the roles of Mary and Elizabeth are inverted. In *The Secrets of Mary Bowser*, for instance, Mary is depicted as taking the initiative in intelligence gathering. She upstages the boastful, somewhat witless and ineffectual Elizabeth—a travesty, in short, of Van Lew's actual historical role. *A Special Friendship*, likewise, gives us a heroic but vulnerable woman, who comes under suspicion, falls into a counter-espionage trap, and has to be saved by the resourceful Mary. In *An Extraordinary Union*, Ellen's independent agency is made even more explicit, since the woman operating undercover in a Confederate household is accountable only to superiors miles away from the scene of her operations. In *A Hope Divided,* Sarah Lynch, the Van Lew figure in Cole's trilogy, is kept totally in the dark about the heroine's activities, as Marlie hides an escaped prisoner in Sarah's own house without her knowledge.

The effect in each case is to ascribe greater autonomy to the heroine, making of her an agent who functions on her own terms, largely free of restraint, and able to bend events to her will. A hero of popular fiction or film is not supposed to be helplessly at the mercy of events. The relationship between Mary and her benefactor, compounded partly of gratitude, resentment, and respect for Elizabeth as a surrogate parent, whereby Elizabeth is perceived at times as a suffocating influence, almost an oppressor, goes largely unexamined. (Cole, in her portrayal of the relations between Marlie and Sarah in *A Hope Divided*, probably comes closest to exploring such complexities.)

The character of Thomas McNiven undergoes some curious transformations in fictional portrayals. In *An Extraordinary Union*, as we have seen, he has morphed into the Scottish Pinkerton agent Malcolm McCall, who becomes Ellen's lover. In the film *A Special Friendship*,

"Quaker" (McNiven's actual codename), persuades Elizabeth Van Lew to work for his spy ring. Possibly drawing on McNiven's own statement, "The rebels got very suspicious of me in January of 1865," and his claim that they subjected him to "rough" interrogation, Quaker in the film falls into the clutches of the Confederate police. Unlike the historical McNiven, who had the sense to take himself out of Richmond when the authorities began closing in, Kenneth Cavander's McNiven character ends up being tortured in custody, and portrayed as a helpless victim of Confederate brutality.

Lois Leveen's portrait in *The Secrets of Mary Bowser* probably comes closest to what we know of the historical McNiven from his own account of himself—in particular the sometimes questionable methods of an agent in wartime. Leveen draws on McNiven's own accounts of orchestrating bread riots and encouraging Richmond munitions workers to cause deadly explosions. Her fictional character even poses as a slave-trader, to give slaves awaiting sale at auction a chance to break away from captivity and reach the Union lines—something the historical McNiven never claimed to have done, although such activities might seem to be in keeping with the rest of what we know of him.

All her life, Mary Richards moved in an atmosphere of religious piety—something not unusual for anyone living in America in the nineteenth century. Even a slave-trader, or the most pitiless plantation overseer, had to find some way of squaring his evil deeds with God's approval. Mary had grown up in a household where religion and Christian charity mattered greatly, followed by schooling that prepared her for the work of a missionary. That her childhood faith, after a time when it seems she claimed to be "no Christian," found a new channel in the Catholic church should hardly be surprising to anyone. Only Leveen, though, really addresses this aspect of Richards' complex personality. Leveen's Mary has been assured by her mother that God has destined her for some special mission. "Do You really have a plan for me?" Mary asks Jesus when her way forward in life seems unclear.[9] Moreover, *The Secrets of Mary Bowser* convincingly depicts Mary's struggle to square Christian pacifism with the call to the enslaved to take up arms for their liberation.

The historical Mary made her most important contribution to the Union war effort by staying faithful to her post in the White House of the Confederacy, and quietly using her eyes and ears. The fictional narratives, bent as they are to fit the demands and conventions of Hollywood-style movies and romantic novels, constantly run the risk of being simplified into crude melodrama, erasing the complexities, psychological challenges, and personal conflicts over role and identity suggested in what we know of Mary Richards' actual life.

It would be interesting to see a film or novel about Richards that focused more closely on the actual details of her story—quite dramatic enough in themselves. As well as her experience of schooling in the North, marked by passionate debates among young scholars about abolition and slavery in the vibrant black community on Witherspoon Street, there is the culture shock of her arrival in Liberia and the challenge of working there, and the brutal awakening of her return to Richmond and subsequent arrest. These events offer promising dramatic material. Mary's time in the Davis household could also be developed in depth, focusing on the psychological drama of her interactions with different members of the household, with an atmosphere of mounting tension as her activities start to arouse suspicion. Her postwar life as a teacher in Georgia, set against a background of racist violence, has never been dealt with in fiction. Her two later failed marriages should also offer interesting material, and Mary's decision to make her way to the North again, and carve out a new life for herself in New York.

There are, of course, other ways to commemorate a life apart from in fiction and apocryphal tales on the internet. Since writing *The Secrets of Mary Bowser*, Professor Lois Leveen has written a number of research-based articles in *The Los Angeles Review of Books*, *The New York Times*, and the *Atlantic Monthly*. She is said to be working on a full-length biography based on her research. I could not end the present work without acknowledging my own debt to the careful and often illuminating findings of this dedicated scholar.[10]

In 1995, the U.S. government paid tribute to "Mary Elizabeth Bowser" by inducting her into the U.S. Military Intelligence Hall of Fame in Fort Huachuca, Arizona. (Besides calling her by her old married name of Bowser, they managed to give her an incorrect middle name. Still, we must recognize that the intention was good.) At the induction ceremony, her contribution in the field of intelligence work was described as follows:

Ms. Bowser certainly succeeded in a highly dangerous mission to the great benefit of the Union effort. She was one of the highest placed and most productive espionage agents of the Civil War.... [Her information] greatly enhanced the Union's conduct of the war.

A number of commemorative plaques and inscriptions have been set up in places associated with Mary Richards. In 1977, a plaque (naming Richards as "Mary Bowser," as is often the case) was placed on a tree in West Farms Soldiers' Cemetery in the Bronx, New York City. In 2021, a new sign commemorating her was erected alongside a Virginia state highway. According to Jen Loux, director of Virginia's highway marker program,

"Markers are not in the same category as monuments or memorial plaques.... They're not intended to honor their subjects, they're intended to educate the public."[11] All the same, despite this disclaimer, the marker is a way of reminding passers-by that Mary Richards existed, and of what she accomplished. A sign can also be found in Richmond, where the Van Lew mansion once stood. This sign for a Virginia History Trails Official Site—SA 69—stands just 400 feet from the St. John's Episcopal church. It commemorates both Richards and Elizabeth Van Lew. The story of "Mary Jane Richards" (Virginia History, at least, gets her name right for once) is said to "parallel that of legendary spy Mary Elizabeth Bowser." And Mary Richards is described, accurately and appropriately, not as Elizabeth Van Lew's servant or dependent, but as her "associate."

Close to the official History Trails signboard lies another reminder of Mary Richards, at the base of a statue outside the Bellevue Elementary School. This older memorial was put in place in 1994 by the Virginia Business and Professional Women's Foundation, and the Virginia Foundation for the Humanities and Public Policy. The inscription reads: "Women of Virginia Historic Trail Honors Mary Elizabeth Bowser."

In the absence of any known grave site, Mary Richards now has a memorial stone in a Richmond cemetery.[12] Commissioned by Virginia historian Veronica A. Davis, memorial number 111467930 can be found at plot 23 (Section G) in Richmond's Woodland Cemetery. Carved on it is her epitaph:

> SHE RISKED HER LIFE AND LIBERTY
> SO THAT ALL COULD KNOW FREEDOM

The People in Mary Richards' World

REVEREND CHARLES BEECHER (1815–1900)

Educator and clergyman, and brother of the novelist Harriet Beecher Stowe. He admired Mary Richards' statuesque appearance—a "Juno" in "somber marble," he called her. He also remarked on her expressive features, and bright, intelligent eyes. He promised to appeal for donations for books for her school. Beecher would be appointed state superintendent of public instruction in Florida (1871–73).

WILSON BOWSER

Mary's first husband. He was, like Mary, a servant of the Van Lew family. The couple were married in 1861, in St. John's Episcopal church, the day before Virginia voted to secede from the United States. The marriage seems not to have lasted.

CAROLINE

An enslaved woman, hired out to work as a cook in the Van Lews' household. She may have been the mother of Mary Richards. (Mary's father was probably a member of the Richards branch of the Van Lew family, but Mary would never have known for certain who her parents were.)

JEFFERSON DAVIS (1808–1889)

President of the Confederacy, 1861–65. Mary Richards worked in his house in Virginia, posing as an illiterate slave to gain information of use to the Union cause. Davis was captured by federal troops in Georgia in May 1865 in the company of his family. It was proposed to try him for treason, but after two years' imprisonment, he was bailed, and eventually pardoned.

VARINA HOWELL DAVIS (1826–1906)

Jefferson Davis's wife always denied that an "educated" black woman had worked in her home and spied there for the Union. But her household staff in Richmond changed constantly and Mary was working hard at pretending to be illiterate. Varina, in any case, delegated the running of the household to her steward, Edward Eggeling, and to the Irish housekeeper Mary O'Melia. Servants in the house constantly came and went during the war, and she may not have kept track.

JOHN DENMAN

The third of Mary's husbands in what seems to have been another short-lived marriage. Denman was a cavalryman with an army unit stationed in Atlanta. He probably was the main reason why Mary tried to petition the Freedmen's Bureau for a new teaching post in Atlanta. By March 1870, Denman had left the army and married someone else—seemingly without telling Mary. When she wrote to Elizabeth Van Lew at the end of October that year, Mary was still signing herself "Mary Denman," apparently unaware that there was a new claimant to that surname.

MAJOR GILBERT L. EBERHART (1830–1907)

Major Eberhart was superintendent of education for the Freedmen's Bureau, Georgia—in effect, Mary Richards' boss when she established her new school in St. Marys after the war. He was an important, if not always sympathetic, figure in her life at that time. She turned to him for both moral and material support, and was often disappointed in him on both counts.

MR. GARVIN

Nothing beyond a surname is known about this man who briefly became Mary Richards' second husband, according to her correspondence with Gilbert Eberhart. His first name, occupation, race, place and date of birth, are all lost to us. We know only that while living and working in St. Marys, Georgia, Mary briefly became Mrs. Mary Richards Garvin. Mr. Garvin then left Georgia for the West Indies, or so he told Mary. After that, he seems to have disappeared from her life.

REVEREND CRAMMOND KENNEDY (1842–1918)

Corresponding secretary of the New York Freedmen's Union commission, Kennedy visited Richards' school and was impressed by what he saw there, and by what Mary told him of her life story. He wrote an article about her in *The American Freedman*, appealing for support for her school, and personally arranged for books to be sent to her.

Dr. Augustus Mitchell

Local physician Dr. Mitchell was supportive and encouraging of Richards' school project in St. Marys. He may also have been the doctor Mary mentioned several times in connection with her chronic ill health while in Georgia. Although he had served as an army surgeon in the Confederate forces during the Civil War, Mitchell received a death threat from hostile whites—possibly because of his employment by the Freedmen's Bureau and his friendship with Mary Richards, the local black schoolteacher.

Thomas McNiven (1835–1904)

Another key member of Richmond's pro-Union underground resistance, McNiven ran his network of agents from a bakery, which he used as a front for his activities. Collaboration with Elizabeth Van Lew led him into contact with Mary Richards. If he referred to her somewhat patronizingly as "little Mary," he still showed deep admiration for her competence as a spy—in particular for her almost total recall of anything she read. McNiven seems to have been the origin of the legend of Richards' "photographic mind."

Betsey Stockton (c. 1798–1865)

After Mary began her education in Princeton, New Jersey, she must have crossed paths with this formidable but caring woman, known to everyone in Princeton's black community. Stockton, herself a former slave, had been a missionary in Hawaii, and was a pillar of educational efforts among the black children of the Witherspoon Street neighborhood. Like her colleague Cecilia Van Tyne (1813–1886), who had been a missionary in Liberia, she set the local youth an example of Christian service, mainly to be performed through the Presbyterian church. It was women like these whom Mary would have been told she must grow up to emulate.

Harriet Beecher Stowe (1811–1896)

The famous author of *Uncle Tom's Cabin* was traveling through Georgia in the company of Crammond Kennedy and her brother Charles when they paid a visit to Mary Richards and her school. Like Kennedy, Stowe expressed admiration for Richards, in particular for her "courage, energy and adroitness" as an agent during the Civil War.

Christopher Taylor

A free black man who drove the wagon for the McNiven bakery, "Chris" probably had more contact with Mary Richards than his employer did, stopping to chat with her when he came to the Davis house to make deliveries. He carried intelligence from her to McNiven and Elizabeth Van Lew as he continued on his rounds.

ELIZA (BAKER) VAN LEW (1798–1875)

Eliza, a descendant of prominent Philadelphia abolitionists and a woman who thought for herself on ethical issues, decided to disobey her husband's instructions in his will regarding the family slaves. John had decreed they were to be retained in bondage, and inherited by his descendants. Eliza freed them, including the child Mary Richards. When Mary was jailed for going out in public without the pass all blacks were required to carry, Eliza attended court to pay a fine on behalf of her alleged "slave." Eliza was later quietly supportive of her daughter Elizabeth's work on behalf of the Union side in the Civil War.

ELIZABETH VAN LEW (1818–1900)

Possibly the most significant person in Mary Richards' life, it was to Elizabeth that Mary wrote when, at the age of thirty, she found herself alone in New York. The older woman was a surrogate parent to Mary, a benefactor, patron, employer, and during the Civil War, a spymaster. Upon the outbreak of war, Elizabeth enlisted Mary in her intelligence network, in which both women performed valuable service for the Union. At the same time, the unequal power relationship between these two strong-minded people led to tensions. Mary would always struggle to assert her independence of Elizabeth, while still feeling a need for her friendship. After the war, for her wartime services to the Union, Elizabeth was appointed Richmond's postmaster general by President Grant's administration. She did well in the post but was driven from it by place-seeking opportunists envious of her success. She was labeled a traitor and ostracized from Richmond society. She ended her days in relative poverty.

JOHN VAN LEW (1790–1843)

When Mary Richards was born, John, a well-to-do hardware merchant, was legally her owner. If he had had his way, she would have continued in slavery. He left directions in his will for all the family slaves to be inherited by various Van Lew relatives.

EDMUND ASA WARE (1837–1885)

Gilbert Eberhart's successor in Georgia from August 1867 onwards. He would become the first president of Atlanta University. Mary wrote to Ware for help in securing a new teaching post near Atlanta—something Ware apologetically told her he was unable to do, while offering to put her name on a waiting list.

ANNA WHITLOCK

Cousin of Elizabeth Van Lew. She speculated that the hired cook named Caroline might have been the mother of Mary Richards.

REVEREND ANTHONY WILLIAMS (1799–1860)

Almost nothing is known about the people Mary stayed with in Liberia, whose direction she worked under there, or who was responsible for her welfare. But when she was miserable and wanted to leave the country, it was to this Liberian former vice-president and Methodist preacher that Elizabeth Van Lew turned for help in bringing Mary home. He seems to have known all about her, and may have been acting as some kind of guardian for her.

Mary Richards' Biographical Timeline

1840: Mary Richards is born a slave in Richmond, Virginia, in the wealthy Van Lew family.

May 17, 1846: Mary is baptized at St. John's Episcopal church.

c. 1847: Now considered a free person by the Van Lews, Mary is sent to Princeton, New Jersey, to receive an education not available to her in the slave-owning South. She is told that it has been decided she will become a missionary.

December 24, 1855: Having completed her education, she sails from New York to Liberia on the *Lamartine*, to begin work as a missionary and teacher.

September 1859: Ill and miserable in Liberia, and having somehow offended her guardians there, Mary writes to Elizabeth Van Lew, her patron, begging to be brought home. Elizabeth relents, and sends for her. She lands back in Baltimore on March 5, 1860, and returns to Richmond.

August 20, 1860: Walking alone in Richmond while Elizabeth Van Lew and her mother are out of town, Mary is challenged by a night watchman who demands her "pass." When she fails to produce it, she is arrested and taken to jail. Brought up before the authorities, she gives false names and claims to be a free black person, only visiting Virginia from Liberia, and intending to return there. Elizabeth Van Lew's mother Eliza is summonsed and fined for allowing her "slave" to go out without a pass.

April 12, 1861: The first battle of the Civil War takes place at Fort Sumter, Charleston, South Carolina.

April 16, 1861: Mary Richards marries Wilson Bowser, in St. John's Episcopal church, where she had been baptized fifteen years earlier. (The marriage seems not to have lasted very long.) The day after the wedding, Virginia votes to secede from the United States.

1861/2: Mary begins working with Elizabeth Van Lew in the Unionist resistance to the Confederacy in Richmond. She accompanies Elizabeth to Libby Prison, where the women receive and smuggle out coded messages from Union prisoners of war for delivery to the U.S. military. Mary then goes to work at the Richmond home of the Confederate president, Jefferson Davis, posing as an illiterate slave. While in the "White House of the Confederacy," she gains information of value to the Union war effort. She passes it on to Elizabeth Van Lew, with the aid of Thomas McNiven and his employee Christopher Taylor.

April 1865: Richmond falls to the incoming Union troops. By now, Mary has already left the Davis household and gone to the Union lines where for some months she has been teaching fellow blacks who have escaped from the South, while possibly continuing to work as a spy.

September/October 1865: Using pseudonyms to protect her identity, Mary speaks to audiences in Brooklyn, New York, about her wartime experiences in the South. She returns to teaching full-time, and is involved in founding new freedmen schools—in Virginia, in Florida, and finally in St. Marys, Georgia.

February–June 1867: Mary's letters to her employers at the Freedmen's Bureau document her struggles in maintaining her Georgia school in the face of her students' poverty and the growing threat from white racists.

June 1867: Mary marries a man named Garvin. She asks her employer to address her by her married name. But Garvin leaves St. Marys—apparently for Cuba—and, it seems, is not heard of again. Disappointed by the refusal of the Freedmen's Bureau to support her school, Mary is forced to close, and to seek employment elsewhere.

September 16, 1868: Mary writes to the Freedmen's Bureau, requesting a teaching post in Atlanta. She has married again, this time to a cavalryman named John Denman. She would like a teaching position close to where her husband is posted, but she is told that none is available in that area. She is invited, however, to put her name on a waiting list.

October 31, 1870: Mary Richards (Denman) writes to Elizabeth Van Lew. She is now living in New York, trying to earn money as a seamstress, while hoping to attend college for further training as a teacher. After this, Mary Richards disappears from the historical record.

1977: A memorial to Mary Richards' heroic life is set up in West Farms Soldiers' Cemetery in the Bronx, New York City.

1994: Women of Virginia set up a memorial in Richmond to honor "Mary Bowser."

1995: Under the name of "Mary Elizabeth Bowser," the U.S. government inducts Mary Richards into the U.S. Military Intelligence Hall of Fame in Fort Huachuca, Arizona.

2012: The state of Virginia sets up a highway marker in Richmond, commemorating Mary Richards and Elizabeth Van Lew.

A memorial stone for Richards, commissioned by local historian Veronica Davis, has been placed at Woodland Cemetery, Richmond.

Endnotes

Chapter 1

1 Beymer, "Miss Van Lew," *Harper's Monthly* (June 1911), pp. 86–99.
2 Letter to John Albree (April 25, 1913) in the Van Lew Papers, quoted in Varon, *Southern Lady, Yankee Spy* (2005), p. 270, n. 52.

Chapter 2

1 "Address of Rev. Alexander Crummell, of Liberia," *African Repository* (July 1861), pp. 257, 271.
2 Davison, "A Visit to the Colored People of Princeton," Ann Maria Davison Papers (1814–1861).
3 "Hawaii Once Had A Negro Missionary," *Pacific Commercial Advertiser* (May 12, 1906), p. 21.
4 "Addresses by a Colored Lady and Henry Ward Beecher," *Brooklyn Daily Eagle* (September 25, 1865), p. 1.
5 Camp, et al., "Letters Received by the American Colonization Society," *Journal of Negro History*, 10.2 (April 1925), p. 159.
6 Van Lew letters: to Williams (April 24, 1857); to Hall (April 21, 1859); to McLain (October 2, 1854); to McLain, confiding her anxieties about Mary (September 22, 1859). Manuscript Division, Library of Congress.
7 "Corresponding member." See "Proceedings of the Board of Directors" (January 19, 1859) in *African Repository*, 35.4 (April 1859), p. 101.
8 "Address of Rev. Alexander Crummell, of Liberia" in *African Repository* (July 1861), pp. 257, 271.
9 American Colonization Society, *Information about Going to Liberia* (1848), p. 1.
10 Letters from missionaries: December 11, 1844; March 18, 1850, courtesy of PBA Galleries. See also Peterson, *The Looking-Glass* (1854), reprod. in Moses (ed.), *Liberian Dreams* (1998), p. 47.
11 Negative reports of Liberia: Washington, "Letter from Monrovia" (June 27, 1854), reprod. in Moses, *Liberian Dreams* (1998), p. 206, and Nesbit, *Four Months in Liberia* (1855), pp. 88–89, 100–101.

12　A more favorable account appears in a letter from William Burke to the ACS president, Ralph R. Gurley (July 26, 1858), in American Colonization Society Papers, Manuscript Division, Library of Congress (18), ww.loc.gov. See also American Colonization Society, *Information about Going to Liberia* (1848), p. 3; Tyler-McGraw, *An African Republic* (2009), reprod. in Camp, et al., "Letters Received by the American Colonization Society," *Journal of Negro History*, 10.2 (April 1925), p. 161; and Williams, *Four Years in Liberia* (1857), reprod. in Moses, *Liberian Dreams* (1998), p. 132.

13　Akpan, "Alexander Crummell and his African 'Race-Work:' An Assessment of His Contributions in Liberia to Africa's 'Redemption,' 1853–1873," *Historical Magazine of the Protestant Episcopal Church*, 45.2 (June 1976), pp. 177–79. For the negative image of the indigenous people of Liberia, see, for example, American Colonization Society, *Proceedings of a Meeting Held at Princeton, New Jersey, July 14, 1848, to form a Society in the State of New Jersey* (1824).

Chapter 3

1　For this statement, and Mary's account of the Van Lew family's hiding of her papers, see "Richmonia Richards," *The Anglo-African* (October 7, 1865), p. 2, c. 4. An earlier talk in New York is recorded in "Addresses by a Colored Lady and Henry Ward Beecher," *Brooklyn Daily Eagle* (September 25, 1865), p.1, c. 2. Richards' account of clandestine wartime meetings at the Van Lew house and Elizabeth Van Lew's "No Unionists here" quote are also summarized in the *Brooklyn Daily Eagle* piece.

2　Quoted in Ryan (ed.), *A Yankee Spy in Richmond* (2001), p. 32.

3　Varina Davis, *Jefferson Davis, A Memoir: By His Wife*, vol. 2 (1890), p. 10.

4　Van Lew in Ryan (ed.), *op. cit.*, pp. 31–32, 36. For Van Lew's change of heart regarding immediate action to end slavery, see *Ibid.*, p. 33, and Varon, *Southern Lady, Yankee Spy* (2005), p. 49.

5　Van Lew in Ryan (ed.), *op. cit.*, p. 32.

6　For these names of Union agents, I am indebted to Varon, *op. cit.*, p. 164. Van Lew's alleged deliberately odd behavior is described by Beymer in "Miss Van Lew," *Harper's Monthly Magazine*, 123 (June 1911), pp. 86–99.

7　Varon, *op. cit.*, p. 89, and Van Lew in Ryan (ed.), *op. cit.*, p. 27.

8　Beymer, *op. cit.*, pp. 86–99.

9　Van Lew in Ryan (ed.), *op. cit.*, p. 43.

10　Beymer, *op. cit.*, pp. 86–99.

Chapter 4

1　See letter to Lieutenant Colonel J. Critcher (May 26, 1863) in *War of the Rebellion*, Serial 040, p. 0826, N. VA., W. VA., MD., and PA. Chapter XXXVII, ehistory.osu.edu.

2　As told by Beymer in "Miss Van Lew," *Harper's Monthly* (June 1911), pp. 86–99.

3　Varina Davis, *Jefferson Davis, A Memoir: By His Wife*, vol. 2 (1890), pp. 79–80, 163, 199.

4　Clinton (ed.), *Mary Chesnut's Diary* (2011), pp. 33–34.

5   Jefferson Davis, *The Rise and Fall of the Confederate Government*, vol. 1 (1881), pp. 261–62. Davis's argument about "penitentiaries and workhouses" occurs in a prewar speech in the U.S. Senate, as reported in the *Congressional Globe* (1860), p. 917. The abolition campaigner W. H. Goodell pointed out the essentially dehumanizing nature of slavery, regardless of how the individual slave might be treated: "The question of slavery or emancipation is not a question of cruel treatment or of kind treatment—of starvation or of full feeding. It is a question whether a man is to be recognized as a man, or a brute—a person or a thing—a spiritual, a moral being, or a mere lump of matter." *The American slave code in theory and practice* (1853), p. 378.

6   "Addresses by a Colored Lady and Henry Ward Beecher," *Brooklyn Daily Eagle* (September 25, 1865), p.1, c. 2.

7   Jefferson Davis, *op. cit.*, pp. 215, 216.

8   Varina Davis, *op. cit.*, pp. 111, 18–19, 183.

9   Clinton (ed.), *op. cit.*, p. 263.

10 "A wary welcome": Varina Davis, *op. cit.*, pp. 202, 203; "Parsimony": *Ibid.*, pp. 160–61.

11 "Addresses by a Colored Lady and Henry Ward Beecher," *Brooklyn Daily Eagle* (September 25, 1865), p. 1, c. 2.

12 Van Lew in Ryan (ed.), *A Yankee Spy in Richmond* (2001), p. 94.

Chapter 5

1   All quotations in this chapter are from the five-page McNiven memoir, transcribed by McNiven's grandson, Robert W. Waitt: *Recollections of Thomas McNiven and his activities in Richmond during the American Civil War*: Personal Papers Collection, Virginia State Library and Archives, Richmond, Virginia, Accession No. 33673.

Chapter 6

1   Clinton (ed.), *Mary Chesnut's Diary* (2011), pp. 248, 216.

2   Richmond citizens' improvisations: Varina Davis, *Jefferson Davis, A Memoir: By His Wife*, vol. 2 (1890), pp. 209–211; sale of the slaves: *Ibid.*, p. 529.

3   "Jeff Davis's Coachman," *Harper's Weekly* (June 7, 1862), p. 365; "Jeff Davis's Coachman," *New York Tribune* (May 24, 1862), p. 8.

4   The contribution was published in *The Anglo-African* (August 6, 1864) under the pseudonym "Africano," and quoted in Ripley et al. (eds.), *Witness for Freedom* (1993), pp. 232–33. Fremont later withdrew from the presidential race.

5   Clinton (ed.), *op. cit.*, p. 248.

6   *Daily South Carolinian* (February 20, 1864), quoted in Stark, "Living with the Enemy: The Jefferson Davis Family and their Servants," *American History* (April 2006), reprod. on historynet.com.

7   Varina Davis, *op. cit.*, pp. 218–19.

8   It was not unknown, however, for free blacks to find themselves conscripted by the Union troops as construction workers and servants.

9   Jefferson Davis, *Rise and Fall of the Confederate Government* (1881), pp. 261–62.

10   Public hanging of the Union spy, Spencer Deaton: *Richmond Examiner* (February 20, 1864); "… used to giving way to wrath": Van Lew in Ryan (ed.), *A Yankee Spy in Richmond* (2001), pp. 65–67.

11   "A climate of fear prevailed": *Ibid.*, pp. 31–32, 36; "No action to be taken": Varon, *Southern Lady, Yankee Spy* (2005), pp. 178–80.

12   "Hanging of Amy Spain," *Harper's Weekly* (September 30, 1865) p. 613; "Amy Spain," *Charleston Courier* (October 7, 1865).

13   Varina Davis, *op. cit.*, pp. 206, 497.

14   Clinton (ed.), *op. cit.*, pp. 227–28.

15   *Ibid.*, p. 283.

16   Varina Davis, *op. cit.* p. 577.

17   Van Lew in Ryan (ed.), *op. cit.*, p. 104.

18   Beymer, "Miss Van Lew," *Harper's Monthly* (June 1911), pp. 86–99; Varon, *Southern Lady, Yankee Spy* (2005), p. 196.

Chapter 7

1   "Addresses by a Colored Lady and Henry Ward Beecher," *Brooklyn Daily Eagle* (September 25, 1865), p. 1, c. 2.

2   "Richmonia Richards," *The Anglo-African* (October 7, 1865), p. 2, c. 4.

Chapter 8

1   Letter from William T. Sherman to Henry W. Halleck (December 24, 1864), cwnc.omeka.chass.ncsu.edu.

2   Clinton (ed.), *Mary Chesnut's Diary* (2011), pp. 311–12, 335.

3   Letter to *The Weekly Anglo-African* (June 25, 1865), reprod. in Ripley, et al. (eds.), *Witness for Freedom* (1993), p. 247.

4   See Reidy, *From Slavery to Agrarian Capitalism in the Cotton Plantation South* (1992), p. 173, and *New Georgia Encyclopedia* at www.georgiaencyclopedia. org.

5   All letters in this chapter, including those of Mary Richards, are from the archives of the United States Freedmen's Bureau: Records of the Superintendent of Education and of the Division of Education, 1865–1872, familysearch.org; Georgia: Roll 8, Letters received, 1–449, Sept 1865–July 1867, images 993 of 1483. Washington D.C.: National Archives and Records Administration, 1969–1978.

6   "Letter from Reverend Crammond Kennedy," *The American Freedman*, 2.1 (April 1867), p. 196.

7   Johnson, "A Black Teacher and Her School in Reconstruction Darien: the Correspondence of Hettie Sabattie and J. Murray Hoag, 1868–1869," *Georgia Historical Quarterly*, 75.1 (Spring 1991), pp. 90–105.

8   Robert Hamilton, editorial in *The Weekly Anglo-African* (September 9, 1865). See also, Young, "Roads to Travel: A Historical Look at the Freedman's Torchlight," *Journal of Black Studies*, 31.5 (May 2001), pp. 671–98.

9   Cimbala and Harris, *Under the Guardianship of the Nation* (1997), p. 13.

10 "Letter from Reverend Crammond Kennedy," *American Freedman*, 2.1 (April 1867), p. 205. See also "a wonderful history" in the same letter. For Charles Beecher's description of Mary Richards, see Charles Beecher's diary (1867). For Stowe's account of her meeting with Richards, see Stowe, "Letter from Florida," quoted in Foster, "Early Tourism and Harriet Beecher Stowe: The Discovery of Stowe's First Published Descriptions of Florida," *Florida Historical Quarterly*, 95.4 (Spring 2017), pp. 480–81.

Chapter 9

1   Cimbala and Harris, *Under the Guardianship of the Nation* (1997).
2   "Ku Klux Klan in the Reconstruction Era," *New Georgia Encyclopedia*.
3   When was Richards in prison for four months—and why? When she was arrested in 1860, on her return from Liberia, she was jailed for only a few days. Was she ever arrested on suspicion of spying? Political detainees were not usually held in the common jail in Richmond, but taken to Castle Thunder. Unless she was simply exaggerating to impress Eberhart with her toughness, we are faced here with yet another mysterious gap in the events of Mary Richards' life.

Chapter 10

1   For this information about Mary Richards' third marriage, I am indebted to Lois Leveen's article, "The Vanishing Black Woman Spy Reappears," *Los Angeles Review of Books* (June 19, 2019). Richards' letter to Van Lew found its way to Cowan's auction rooms, where it was brought to Leveen's attention.
2   Van Lew in Ryan (ed.), *A Yankee Spy in Richmond* (2001), pp. 129, 132.

Chapter 11

1   "The spy who set fire to the Confederate White House," shesmagicblog. wordpress.com.
2   "Call Me Bond. Ellen Bond," *Good Witches, Bad Bitches*, Episode 41, gwbbpodcast.com. Also, Heichelbech, R., "The First Bond Spy Was a Black Woman Working for the Union," liveplayeat.com: "Mary Bowser assumed the name of Ellen Bond in order to lead her double life as a spy."
3   Abbott, *Liar, Temptress, Soldier, Spy* (2014), pp. 252–53.
4   "The Spy Who Served Me," *Morning Edition*, National Public Radio (April 19, 2002), 12:00 a.m., Eastern Time.
5   Leveen, "The Vanishing Black Woman Spy Reappears," *Los Angeles Review of Books* (June 19, 2019).
6   "Women ... have a far greater capacity for cool and lonely courage than men," quoted from Wood, "Interview with Selwyn Jepson" (March 7, 1986).
7   Grande, "Catching up with Ted Lange from the Love Boat," *Zoomer* (January 13, 2017), everythingzoomer.com.
8   Russnow, "Lady Patriot at the Hudson: Ted Lange Has Come a Long Way from The Love Boat" (December 9, 2012), huffpost.com.
9   Leveen, *The Secrets of Mary Bowser* (2012), p. 87.

10   See, for example, "A Black Spy in the Confederate White House," *New York Times* (June 21, 2012); "The Spy Photo that Fooled NPR, the U.S. Army Intelligence Center, and Me," *The Atlantic* (June 27, 2013); "The Spy Photo that Fooled NPR, the U.S. Army Intelligence Center, and Me," *The Atlantic* (June 27, 2013).

11   Scribner, "Set to Mark 'Union Spy,' Virginia Combats Self-Made Myths," *VPM News* (May 19, 2021).

12   The gravestone was commissioned and the epitaph composed by Virginia historian Veronica A. Davis, author of *Here I Lay My Burdens Down* (2000).

Bibliography

Manuscript Collections

American Colonization Society Papers, Manuscript Division, Library of Congress (18), ww.loc.gov
Charles Beecher, diary (1867): unpublished holding, Harriet Beecher Stowe Center, Hartford, Connecticut
Ann Maria Davison Papers (1814–1861): MC 234, folder 22, Schlesinger Library, Radcliffe Institute, Harvard University, Cambridge, MA
Abraham Lincoln papers, U.S. Library of Congress: hdl.loc.gov
Letters from missionaries: December 11, 1844; March 18, 1850, courtesy of PBA Galleries
McNiven memoir, *Recollections of Thomas McNiven and his activities in Richmond during the American Civil War*: Personal Papers Collection, Virginia State Library and Archives, Richmond, Virginia, Accession No. 33673
"United States, Freedmen's Bureau, Records of the Superintendent of Education and of the Division of Education, 1865–1872," database with images: familysearch. org
March 9, 2015, Georgia, Roll 8, Letters received, 1–449, September 1865–July 1867, image 993 of 1483; citing multiple NARA microfilm publications. Washington D.C.: National Archives and Records Administration, 1969–1978
Van Lew correspondence: Elizabeth Van Lew Papers, Library of Virginia, Richmond (microfilm edition); and original manuscript, New York Public Library

Books

Abbott, K., *Liar, Temptress, Soldier, Spy: Four Women Undercover in the Civil War* (New York: Harper Collins, 2014)
American Colonization Society, *Information about Going to Liberia: Things which Every Emigrant to Liberia Ought to Know. Common Objections to Going to Liberia Answered. Reply to Certain Cavilings Against Colonization* (Washington: Alexander, 1848)

—, *Proceedings of a Meeting Held at Princeton, New Jersey, July 14, 1848, to form a Society in the State of New Jersey to Cooperate with the American Colonization Society* (Princeton, NJ: D. A. Borrenstein, 1824)

Cimbala, P. A., with Harris, W. C., *Under the Guardianship of the Nation: The Freedmen's Bureau and the Reconstruction of Georgia, 1865–1870* (Athens, GA: University of Georgia Press, 1997)

Clinton, C., (ed.), *Mary Chesnut's Diary* (New York: Penguin, 2011)

Cole, A., *An Extraordinary Union* (New York: Kensington Books, 2017)

—, *A Hope Divided* (New York: Kensington Books, 2017)

—, *An Unconditional Freedom* (New York: Kensington Books, 2019)

Davis, J., *Rise and Fall of the Confederate Government* (Public Domain Books, n.d.)

Davis, V., *Jefferson Davis, A Memoir: By His Wife*, vols. 1 and 2 (New York: Belford, 1890)

Davis, Veronica A., *Here I Lay My Burdens Down: A History of the Black Cemeteries of Richmond, Virginia* (Richmond: Dietz Press, 2000)

Goodell, W. H., *The American slave code in theory and practice: Its distinctive features shown by its statues, judicial decisions, and illustrative facts* (New York: American and Foreign Anti-slavery Society, 1853)

Jones, J. B., *A Rebel War Clerk's Diary at the Confederate States Capital*, vol. 2 (Philadelphia: Lippincott, 1866)

Lange, T., *Lady Patriot*, (Bloomington, Indiana: Trafford Publishing, 2013)

Leveen, L., *The Secrets of Mary Bowser* (New York: Hodder & Stoughton, 2012)

Markle, D. E., *Spies and Spymasters of the Civil War* (New York: Hippocrene, 2004)

Moses, W. J., (ed.), *Liberian Dreams: Back-to-Africa Narratives from the 1850s* (University Park: Pennsylvania State UP, 1998)

Olusoga, D., *Black and British: A Forgotten History* (London: Pan, 2017)

Reidy, J. R., *From Slavery to Agrarian Capitalism in the Cotton Plantation South* (Chapel Hill: University of N. Carolina Press, 1992)

Ripley, C. P., et al., (eds.), *Witness for Freedom: African American Voices on Race, Slavery, and Emancipation* (Chapel Hill: University of N. Carolina Press, 1993)

Ryan, D., (ed.), *A Yankee Spy in Richmond: The Civil War Diary of "Crazy Bet" Van Lew* (Mechanicsburg, PA: Stackpole, 2001)

Tyler-McGraw, M., *An African Republic* (Chapel Hill: University of N. Carolina Press, 2009)

Varon, E., *Southern Lady, Yankee Spy: The True Story of Elizabeth Van Lew: A Union Agent in the Heart of the Confederacy* (Oxford: Oxford University Press, 2005)

Williams, S., *Four Years in Liberia* (Philadelphia: King & Baird, 1857)

Articles, Letters, and Podcasts

"Address of Rev. Alexander Crummell, of Liberia," *African Repository* (July 1861), pp. 257, 271

"Addresses by a Colored Lady and Henry Ward Beecher," *Brooklyn Daily Eagle* (September 25, 1865), p.1, c. 2

Akpan, M. B., "Alexander Crummell and his African 'Race-Work:' An Assessment of His Contributions in Liberia to Africa's 'Redemption,' 1853–1873," *Historical Magazine of the Protestant Episcopal Church*, 45.2 (June 1976), pp. 177–79

Allen, W. E., "Rethinking the History of Settler Agriculture in Nineteenth-Century Liberia," *The International Journal of African Historical Studies*, 37.3 (2004), pp. 435–62

"Amy Spain," *Charleston Courier* (October 7, 1865)

Bell, P., "Editorial," *The San Francisco Elevator* (July 28, 1865)

"Call Me Bond. Ellen Bond," *Good Witches, Bad Bitches,* Episode 41, gwbbpodcast.com

Beymer, "Miss Van Lew," *Harper's Monthly* (June 1911), pp. 86–99.

Camp, A., et al., "Letters Received by the American Colonization Society," *Journal of Negro History*, 10.2 (April 1925)

Davison, A. M., "A Visit to the Colored People of Princeton," Ann Maria Davison Papers

Foster Jr., J. T., "Early Tourism and Harriet Beecher Stowe: The Discovery of Stowe's First Published Descriptions of Florida," *Florida Historical Quarterly*, 95.4 (Spring 2017), pp. 480–81

Grande, L., "Catching up with Ted Lange from the Love Boat," *Zoomer* (January 13, 2017), everythingzoomer.com

"Hanging of Amy Spain," *Harper's Weekly* (September 30, 1865)

"Hawaii Once Had A Negro Missionary," *Pacific Commercial Advertiser* (May 12, 1906), p. 21

Heichelbech, R., "The First Bond Spy Was a Black Woman Working for the Union," liveplayeat.com

"Jeff Davis's Coachman," *Harper's Weekly* (June 7, 1862), p. 365

"Jeff Davis's Coachman," *New York Tribune* (May 24, 1862), p. 8

"Jefferson Davis's Coachman," *National Anti-Slavery Standard* (May 24, 1862), p. 3

Johnson, W. B., "A Black Teacher and Her School in Reconstruction Darien: the Correspondence of Hettie Sabattie and J. Murray Hoag, 1868–1869," *Georgia Historical Quarterly*, 75.1 (Spring 1991), pp. 90–105

Klebaner, B. J., "American Manumission Laws and the Responsibility for Supporting Slaves," *Virginia Magazine of History and Biography*, 63.4 (October 1955), pp. 443–53

"Letter from Reverend Crammond Kennedy," *The American Freedman*, 2.1 (April 1867), p. 205

Letter from Robert E. Lee to Lieutenant Colonel J. Critcher (May 26, 1863), *War of the Rebellion*: Serial 040, p. 0826, N. VA, W. VA, MD, and PA, Chapter 37, ehistory.osu.edu

"Letters Received by the American Colonization Society," *Journal of Negro History*, 10.2 (April 1925), p. 159

Letter from William T. Sherman to Henry W. Halleck (December 24, 1864), cwnc. omeka.chass.ncsu.edu

Leveen, L., "A Black Spy in the Confederate White House," *New York Times* (June 21, 2012)

—, "The Spy Photo that Fooled NPR, the U.S. Army Intelligence Center, and Me," *The Atlantic* (June 27, 2013)

—, "The Vanishing Black Woman Spy Reappears," *Los Angeles Review of Books* (June 19, 2019)

"Proceedings of the Board of Directors" (January 19, 1859), *African Repository*, 35.4 (April 1859), p. 101

"Richmonia Richards," *The Anglo-African* (October 7, 1865), p. 2, c. 4

Russnow, M., "Lady Patriot at the Hudson: Ted Lange Has Come a Long Way from The Love Boat" (December 9, 2012), huffpost.com

Scribner, C., "Set to Mark 'Union Spy,' Virginia Combats Self-Made Myths," *VPM News* (May 19, 2021)

Stark, M., "Living with the Enemy: The Jefferson Davis Family and their Servants," *American History* (April 2006), historynet.com

Wood, C., "Interview with Selwyn Jepson" (March 7, 1986), Imperial War Museum, #9331 iwm.org.uk/collections

Young, P. A., "Roads to Travel: A Historical Look at the Freedman's Torchlight," *Journal of Black Studies*, 31.5 (May 2001), pp. 671–98

Films

Cook, F., with Cavander, K., *A Special Friendship*, CBS network (March 31, 1987)

Stone, M. P., (director and scriptwriter), *Ellen Bond, Secret Agent* (movie trailer) (Written in Stone Productions, 2018)

Index